Gout Hater's Cookbook

III

The Low Purine Diet Cookbook

by Jodi Schneiter

GOUT HATER'S COOKBOOK III
THE LOW PURINE DIET COOKBOOK

Published by:
Southeast Media Productions
87 Piedmont Drive
Palm Coast, Florida 32164
USA
Phone: 386.206.1163
Fax: 386.586.5564
Website: www.gout-haters.com

Library of Congress Control Number: 2003098074

ISBN-10: 1-888141-87-5
ISBN-13: 978-1-888141-87-0

This book is not intended as a substitute for medical advice. Always consult your physician before making any changes in your diet. The information provided may vary from the advice given to you by your physician or dietitian. As every individual case is different, please follow what has been recommended for you, including diet, medication and exercise.

Many, many thanks to the Purine Research Society and its efforts to help children with purine autism; and to Tahma Metz, whose help has been invaluable.

Special thanks to Nidal Kahl and Biogen Laboratory Developments, LLC for help in testing foods for purine levels.

Special thanks to King Orchards in Central Lakes, Michigan for the contribution of tart cherry juice concentrate for testing recipes.

Table of Contents

Introduction - 4

What is Gout? - 5

Foods Allowed - 6

Foods & Ingredients Not Allowed - 7

Legumes and Complete Proteins - 9

Salicylates - 10

Important Research Results - 11

Additional Notes - 11

Metric Conversions - 13

Using Raw Ingredients vs. MSG - 13

Planning Holiday Dishes - 16

Presentation - 17

Breakfast - 18

Appetizers & Beverages - 26

Dips - 36

Main Dishes - 39

Soups - 61

Sides & Sauces - 64

Salads - 78

Desserts - 85

Basics from Scratch - 102

Index - 111

Helpful Links - 112

INTRODUCTION
Gout Hater's Cookbook III:
The Low Purine Diet Cookbook

Researching the purine values of foods from one publication to another can be frustrating, if not overwhelming. One publication will report that the purine value of a food is low, whereas another will place the same food item in a group of foods higher in purines. To add to the confusion, purines do not all possess the same molecular weight, and do not all yield an identical amount of uric acid in the end product.

Most of the items listed in our "Foods Allowed, Lowest Purine Group" list are reported to contain 50 mg or less of purines per 100 g. The exceptions include broccoli, which was tested to show about 71 mg (placed in foods allowed), and baker's yeast (also placed in foods allowed), which is extremely high in purines. Yeast is only to be used for the purposes of baking, *not* in yeast supplements. When incorporated into a recipe for white bread, the total amount of purines in the end product is acceptable.

It is possible that your dietitian or physician will place you on a modified purine diet, which usually allows for 3-4 ounces per day of meats relatively high in purines, plus any assortment of foods on our "Foods Allowed" list. Included on page 8 are meats considered to be relatively high in purines. These items can be found in the "Foods Allowed [skinless white meat chicken or turkey]" as well as "Foods not Allowed" listings.

However, this book only contains recipes for dishes that are very low in purines. *Gout Hater's Cookbook III* attempts to free you of the "3-4 ounce per day" regimen of meats that are relatively high in purines by offering alternative, stand-alone, delicious recipes using foods lowest in purines.

Featuring an Ovo-Lacto-Vegetarian (milk and eggs allowed) diet that meets the lowest purine requirements, this book is suitable for persons suffering from gout as well as their families and friends.

Likewise, the recipes offered in our book comply with "restricted" as well as "modified" purine diets. However, don't let the word "restricted" make you in any way feel as though you might have an unremarkable list of bland food choices. There is a world of possibilities in creating tasty dishes, using delicious recipes that can be not only pleasing to the palette, but of great assistance on the journey to lowering your uric acid levels.

Please Note: The food lists contained in this book may vary from the list supplied by your own physician. This book is not intended as a substitute for the advice given by your physician. Please be sure to follow your physician's instructions, including diet, medication and exercise.

WHAT IS GOUT?

Gout is a condition that is brought on by an excessive amount of uric acid, an end product of purines, in the body. Excess uric acid in the blood, called hyperurecemia, can occur when the body over-produces uric acid, fails to eliminate it properly, or a combination of both.

Needle-shaped uric acid crystals form in the connective tissue of the joints. As white blood cells rupture when attempting to ingest the crystals, other white blood cells rapidly accumulate, resulting in inflammation and excrutiating pain.

Gout can be brought on by many causes: surgery, some diuretic medications, dehydration, alcohol consumption, extreme changes in diet, use of aspirin (a salicylate), renal insufficiency, trauma, and a diet of foods high in purines. In addition, high acidity in the joint fluid can decrease the solubility of uric acid, thereby increasing the risk of gout.

Attacks of gout can occur with little or no notice, usually in joints of the extremities, such as the large toe, possibly due to the lower body temperature found in these areas.

More than 5.9 million people in the United States suffer from gout, and the numbers are growing. Ninety per cent are men over 40. Gout does not usually occur in women until after menopause.

Treatments include symptom-relieving medicines such as anti-inflammatories and colchicine, preventive medicines such as allopurinol, eliminating alcohol, and a diet of foods lower in purines. Interestingly, gout is said to be the only rheumatic disease known to be helped when certain foods are avoided.

FOODS ALLOWED
GREEN LIGHT - LOWEST PURINE GROUP

Beets (except beet tops), berries, broccoli, carrots, celery, coconuts, corn, cucumbers, fruits and fruit juice, eggplant, green string beans (not bulging), grits, hominy, jicama, leafy greens (except those listed in the moderate level group), leeks, lettuce, okra, olives, onions, parsnips, peppers, potatoes, radishes, rhubarb, sago, squash, tomatoes, turnips, vegetable soups[1], water chestnuts. Nuts (except peanuts - see Legumes, page 9)

Dairy (low fat or fat free): cottage cheese, cheese, eggs (no more than one yolk per day; more than one white is allowed), ice cream, margarine, milk, ricotta, yogurt. Watch the ingredients for xanthan/xanthum gum or xanthine.

Cereals (except whole grain), corn flakes, semolina pasta/macaroni (preferably 100% semolina), white rice, tapioca

White flour (without malted barley flour added), matzoh, white rice flour, arrowroot flour, baker's yeast[2], white bread, French bread, matzoh, plain white bagels (watch for malt), white pita bread

Ketchup, mustard, mayonnaise, honey, sugar

Sodas: non-cola, non-caffeine
Vegetable oils[3]: canola, olive, soy

---

1. Not containing meat stock, meat extracts or high-purine vegetables.
2. Only as a part of baking. Yeast supplements are not allowed.
3. Peanut oil is not allowed.

FOODS ALLOWED (CONTINUED)

YELLOW LIGHT - MODERATE LEVEL PURINE GROUP

The following non-meat items are allowed, but are grouped differently here only because they contain higher purine levels. According to a 12 year study published in the New England Journal of Medicine *(see page 11), a moderate amount of vegetables rich in purines did not increase the risk of gout.*

Artichokes, asparagus, beans, bean sprouts, beet tops, bok choy, Brussels sprouts, cabbage, cauliflower, dried beans and peas, kale, legumes (page 9) lentils, mushrooms, peanuts and peanut butter, peanut oil, peas, soy/soy products (including tofu, soy sauce and soy flour), spinach, Swiss chard

Wheat germ and whole grain cereal or flour, including barley, barley malt, bran, brown rice, oatmeal, oats, rye, pumpernickel, graham flour, malt, whole wheat, whole wheat flour; macaroni products not labeled as semolina or durum semolina

Your system may be able to tolerate 3-4 ounces (about the size of a deck of cards) of the following foods per day (Please check with your physician or dietitian):

Skinless white meat chicken or turkey.

FOODS AND INGREDIENTS
NOT ALLOWED
RED LIGHT - AVOID THESE ITEMS!

The following foods and ingredients are either very high in purines or otherwise not allowed in the restricted purine diet (See "Important Research Results," page 11; "Additional Notes", page 11):

Alcoholic beverages, coffee, tea, chocolate, cocoa, cola drinks, carob, carob bean gum, caffeine

All types of seafood, especially anchovies, caviar, fish roe, herring, ocean perch, sardines, scallops, smelt, sprat, trout and tuna. Seafoods relatively high in purines include cod, crayfish, eel, haddock, lobster, mackerel, oyster, plaice, pike, salmon, shrimp and sole (See "Important Research Results," page 11)

The following meats are very high in purines: game meats, horse, kidney, lamb, meat extracts, muscle, organ meats, sausage, spleen and tongue. The following meats are relatively high in purines, but not recommended, because they are high in saturated fats: beef (brisket, chuck, filet, shoulder, rump, corned beef), dark meat chicken or poultry and poultry skin, pork (bacon, chop, chuck, filet, hind leg, shoulder), meat broth, veal filet or shoulder.

Brewer's yeast, yeast supplements, seeds, MSG, xanthine, xanthan/ xanthum gum, lard, powdered or evaporated milk, whole milk/ whole milk products.

LEGUMES AND COMPLETE PROTEINS

Legumes, although relatively high in purines, have not been shown to increase the risk of gout (However, it is advised that they be eaten in moderation. Please see "Important Research Results," page 11). With the exception of soy, legumes contain incomplete proteins. When eating legumes, various grains such as macaroni, rice, bread, pasta, couscous and corn can be added to your meal in order to make "complimentary proteins." In addition, the combination of the two will help reduce the total purine intake. Following are examples of legumes:

adzuki beans

black beans

black-eyed peas (cowpeas, black-eyed beans)

butter beans

cannellini

chickpeas (garbanzo beans)

cranberry beans (not to be confused with cranberries)

fava beans (broad beans)

flageolets

great northern beans

kidney beans

lentils

lima beans

mung beans

navy beans

peanuts

peas

pinto beans

red beans

soy beans

split peas

white beans

SALICYLATES

Following is a list of some medications containing salicylates, which should be avoided. Salicylates can worsen your condition as well as adversely affect the potency of some medications.

Aspirin
Anacin
Anaflex
Arthritis Pain Formula
Arthropan
Aspergum
Bayer Aspirin
Bufferin
Cope
Doan's Regular Strength Tablets
Ecotrin Empirin
Gensan
Healthprin
Mono-Gesic
Tricosal
Trilisate

A more comprehensive list may be obtained from your doctor or local pharmacist.

IMPORTANT RESEARCH RESULTS

According to a twelve year study published in March of 2004 in the *New England Journal of Medicine*, it is no longer necessary to avoid vegetables that are high in purines. The study states that there was no association found between a *moderate* intake of vegetables high in purines and an increase in the risk of gout.

As reported in the same study, the daily intake of non-fat and low-fat milk and yogurt showed a marked decrease in the risk of attacks. The largest decrease was seen in those who consumed at least 2 servings of non-fat or low-fat milk and/or yogurt each day. This finding corresponds with other reports that showed an increase in uric acid levels due to abstinence from dairy products.

In contrast, eating one serving of meat per day can increase the risk of gout by 21%, and each single serving of seafood during the space of one week can drastically increase the risk of gout!

In addition, men with a higher body mass carried an increased risk, and alcohol consumption posed an increased risk.

ADDITIONAL NOTES

Macaroni or pasta products should be labeled as 100% semolina or durum semolina. 100% semolina is most preferred, although durum semolina is acceptable. 100% durum is considered part of the "Yellow Light - Moderate Level Purine Group". When choosing bread and cereals, check ingredients for malt (yellow light- allowed, but avoiding this ingredient can help reduce your purine intake). When choosing flour, try more refined flours such as pasta flour, Softasilk cake flour or Swans Down cake flour.

Xanthine and xanthan/xanthum gum: When choosing dairy products such as yogurt, cream cheese, ice cream and cottage cheese, watch for xanthine, xanthan/xanthum gum or unspecified gums. Xanthine, a purine base, appears in the metabolism of purines to uric acid. Xanthine and xanthine derivatives can be found in coffee, tea, chocolate and cola drinks, to name only a few. Xanthan gum, not to be confused with xanthine (similar root sound), was tested and found to be very high in purines.

Avoid saturated fats! There are a number of beef, pork and veal cuts (see page 8) that are only relatively high in purines, but they can contain a great deal of saturated fat! Please remember that consuming any meat or seafood servings can increase the risk of gout!

Salicylates (including aspirin) are not allowed. See page 10 for a list of examples of medications containing salicylates.

Green string beans should be used only while the beans are very small and not bulging.

Eggs should be limited to no more than one yolk per day. More than one egg white is acceptable.

Water: drinking water can help the body eliminate uric acid. Try to drink eight to ten 8-ounce glasses of water each day.

Watch for extreme changes in diet. *Moderation is the key in your dieting habits; always make any changes gradually.*

Extracts: When using any type of extract, be sure to use only if the alcohol content will be cooked out. Ingestion of alcohol promotes uric acid production.

Alcohol: Avoid alcohol!!! Not only can alcohol contribute to an attack of gout, it is also possible that the effects of allopurinol are inhibited by alcohol intake.

Nicotine: If you are a smoker, try to reduce your nicotine intake. Nicotine is an extremely toxic substance which affects the central nervous system and causes an increase in heartbeat and breathing rates. When used in conjunction with alcohol, the amount of addiction is said to increase. Related effects include increased blood pressure, which can ultimately be a factor in causing gout.

Attacks of gout can be triggered by a high acidity level in the joint fluids. Taking 3 to 6 grams of sodium bicarbonate per day can help increase the solubility of uric acid. This should be done only under the guidance of your physician.

METRIC CONVERSIONS

1 pound	=	.4536 kg
1 ounce (weight)	=	28.35g
1 cup	=	.2365 liter
2 cups (1 pint)	=	.473 liter
4 cups (1 quart)	=	.946 liter
4 quarts (1 gallon)	=	3.784 liters
1 teaspoon	=	5 ml
1 Tablespoon	=	15 ml
1 fluid ounce (1/8 cup)	=	30 ml

CONVERTING FAHRENHEIT TO CELSIUS

Fahrenheit is converted to degrees Celsius as follows:
1. Begin with degrees Fahrenheit
2. Subtract 32
3. Multiply by 5
4. Divide by 9

USING RAW INGREDIENTS VS. MSG

Glutamic acid appears in two forms - one form occurs naturally; the other is manufactured or processed. The type of glutamic acid which occurs natually in raw ingredients has not been found to cause adverse reactions in humans. MSG, or monosodium glutamate, contains both forms of glutamic acid. Manufactured or processed free glutamic acid is an excitotoxin. It has been reported to cause a multitude of devastating symptoms. These include severe asthma attacks, seizures, psychological disorders and heart arrhythmia, among many others. Laboratory animals tested with manufacured or processed free glutamic acid (MSG) have been reported to develop brain lesions as well as retinal damage.

The safety (or lack thereof) in the use of MSG is a subject of controversy. The Food and Drug Administration (FDA) classifies MSG as a flavor enhancer Generally Recognized as Safe (GRAS), whereas many researchers have reported adverse reactions, time and time again.

To complicate matters, the FDA does not require that "MSG" or "monosodium glutamate" be named on the list of ingredients, unless separately added. For example, one common ingredient found on product labels is "hydrolyzed vegetable protein." This ingredient contains up to 40% MSG. In addition, both hydrolyzed animal and vegetable protein are classified by the FDA as natural ingredients. This is because they began with a natural source, such as pork blood, before going through the fermentation process. Ingredient names such as "natural flavor," flavor," or "spices" are often a legal description of hydrolyzed protein, which contains MSG. Unfortunately, "natural" does not always mean *healthy or nutritious.* For example, oleander and arsenic, both lethal poisons, are "natural."

To further confuse the issue, "spices" could be referring to ground basil leaves, pepper and ground mustard OR hydrolyzed vegetable protein (which contains MSG) OR any combination of these items.

Additional product labels which might indicate that a product contains MSG include *ultra-pasteurized, enzyme modified, protein fortified, fermented,* and *no MSG added.* "No MSG Added" tends to indicate that although ingredients which contain MSG might have been used, no MSG has been separately added.

Sometimes it can be virtually impossible to determine whether a product contains MSG. The struggle to avoid it can be endless, as an overwhelming majority of food products on the market today contain MSG, and the amounts are increasing. Sometimes it seems as though the only defense is to use as many *raw ingredients as possible.* For this reason, you will not see the use of artificial sweeteners such as aspartame, also an excitotoxin, in this cookbook.

**Following is a list of product ingredients
which always contain MSG:**
monosodium glutamate
· monopotassium glutamate
glutamic acid
gelatin
hydrolyzed vegetable or animal protein
sodium caseinate
calcium caseinate
textured vegetable protein
yeast extract

Ingredients which often contain MSG:
barley malt
flavor(s) or flavoring
corn syrup
modified food starch
cornstarch
milk powder
natural flavor(s) or flavoring
bouillon
carrageenan
wheat/rice/oat protein
whey/whey protein/whey protein isolate
spices
soy sauce
gums
yeast nutrients
protease

PLANNING HOLIDAY DISHES

Recipe suggestions for Autumn and Winter holidays:

MAIN DISHES:
Sweet and Sour Eggplant
Squash Casserole
Acorn Squash Souffle
Onion Pie
Egg Sauce over Buttermilk
    Biscuits

STARTERS:
Float Punch
Olive Rolls
Chewy Cheese Puffs
Crunchy Potoato Rolls
Squash Puppies
Ranch Pasta Salad

SIDE DISHES:
Squash Paprika
Cheese Potatoes
Rosemary Potatoes
Pasta Salad
Celery Salad
Baked Macaroni and Cheese

DESSERTS:
Spiced Fruit
Hot Peaches and Cream
Cherry Yogurt
Sweet Raisin Curry Rolls
Blackberry Tartlets
Cherry Mousse

Recipe suggestions for Spring and Summer holidays:

MAIN DISHES:
Welsh Rarebit
Moussaka Casserole
Vegetable Manicotti in
    Lemon Sauce
Baked Chilies Rellenos
Steamed Zucchini Pesto
Tamales
Chef Salad

STARTERS:
Antipasto Salad
Celery with Blue Cheese
    Dressing
Cheese Ball
Sandwich Rolls
Float Punch

SIDE DISHES:
Corn, Tomato & Celery Salad
Tomato Salad
Pasta and Celery Salad
Summer Pasta Salad
Tropical Rice Ring

DESSERTS:
Melon Sorbet
Tart Lime Sherbet
Cherry Slush
Flan
Double Orange Parfait
Strawberry

PRESENTATION

Don't forget that the appearance of your serving dishes can be nine-tenths of the battle when entertaining. Gourmet meals at a five-star restaurant are not necessarily served in large portions, but are typically arranged beautifully on the plate, and are pleasing to the eye as well as to the palette. Keeping the appearance of your dish in mind, even when not entertaining, can also be an enormous help to your own diet, so pamper yourself by preparing your everyday recipes with a nicely arranged dinner plate.

Homemade Margarine

Following is one of the most basic recipes found in every one of *The Gout Hater's Cookbook* collection. Using this recipe (also found on page 108) instead of "store bought" margarine, you are freeing yourself of some of the countless additives that are needlessly ingested every day.

3/4 cup butter, softened

3/4 cup canola oil

1/8 teaspoon salt (optional)

Combine ingredients in a blender. Blend well until smooth. Transfer to airtight containers and refrigerate. To serve, remove from fridge for at least 10 minutes. Makes 1-1/2 cups.

Breakfast

Spiced Vanilla Yogurt

3/4 cup skim milk
2 teaspoons flour
1-1/2 teaspoons vanilla extract
1/2 teaspoon cinnamon
1/4 teaspoon allspice
1/4 teaspoon nutmeg
2 Tablespoons sugar
2 cups plain non fat yogurt
(no xanthan gum)

Combine all ingredients, except yogurt, in a medium saucepan. Stir with a whisk until smooth.

Cook over medium high heat, stirring frequently, for about 10 minutes. This will give the alcohol in the vanilla extract a chance to cook away.

Remove from heat. Chill, then stir into yogurt. Serves 2-3.

Buttermilk Biscuits

2 cups flour
1/2 teaspoon baking soda
1/4 teaspoon salt
4 Tablespoons margarine, melted
3/4 cup low fat buttermilk

Preheat oven to 400 degrees. Lightly mist a cookie sheet with canola oil. Combine flour, baking soda and salt in a large mixing bowl.

Stir with a fork for about 30 seconds, until all ingredients are evenly distributed. Set aside.

Combine margarine with buttermilk, stirring well. Add to flour mixture gradually, stirring first with a fork, and then kneading with floured hands.

Place dough on a lightly floured surface. Pat with damp hands to about 1/2-inch thickness. Cut into 3" rounds, then place on cookie sheet.

For best results, brush with buttermilk. Bake at 400 degrees for about 15 minutes, or until lightly browned. Makes 9 biscuits.

Almond Ginger Biscotti

3 egg whites

3/4 cup sugar

1/2 cup canola oil

1-1/2 teaspoons baking powder

2 teaspoons fresh ginger, finely ground

1 teaspoon vanilla extract

3 cups flour

1 cup chopped almonds

Preheat oven to 350 degrees. Lightly mist a cookie sheet with canola oil. Combine egg whites, sugar, canola oil, baking powder and vanilla extract in a medium mixing bowl. Blend with whisk.

Stir in flour and almonds, then knead with floured hands until no longer sticky. Roll into a loaf 2-3 inches in diameter, dividing into two loaves if desired.

Place on cookie sheet and bake at 350 degrees for 30 minutes.

Remove from oven and allow to cool for 10-

15 minutes. Cut into 3/4 to 1-inch slices with a bread knife.

Replace slices onto cookie sheet, laying the slices on their sides. Return to oven and bake 15-20 more minutes or until browned.

Cool and serve with hot herbal tea. Makes about 2 dozen biscotti.

Creamed Rice

3/4 cup skim milk
1 Tablespoon flour
1-1/2 to 2 cups cooked rice

Combine milk and flour in a small mixing bowl. Stir with a fork or whisk until smooth. Place in a medium saucepan together with rice.

Cook over medium-high heat, stirring constantly, until thickened. Serves 2.

Optional: Serve topped with a dab of preserves or honey.

Parmesan Eggs

3 eggs, one yolk discarded
1-1/2 cups skim milk
1/8 teaspoon pepper
4 ounces grated Parmesan
1/2 teaspoon garlic powder or 2 cloves pressed
garlic
3 cups dry bread, cubed

Preheat oven to 350 degrees. Lightly mist a 13 x 9 x 2 baking dish with canola oil. Set aside.

In a large mixing bowl, beat eggs with whisk for about 30 seconds.

Stir in milk, pepper, Parmesan and garlic powder.

Add bread cubes, tossing until evenly distributed. Transfer to baking dish. Cover. Bake at 350 degrees for 30 minutes.

Uncover and continue baking until top is lightly browned, about 10-15 minutes. Serves 4-6.

Onion and Herb Biscuits

1/3 cup sweet onions, minced
1/4 cup water
2-1/4 cups flour
2 teaspoons baking powder
1/2 teaspoon baking soda
1/4 teaspoon salt
1/8 teaspoon pepper
2 sprigs dill, finely chopped
1 sprig rosemary, finely chopped
2 basil leaves, finely chopped
3/4 cup low fat buttermilk
5-1/2 Tablespoons olive oil

Preheat oven to 400 degrees. Combine onions and water in a small saucepan. Cook until onions are transparent and water is reduced. Set aside to cool.

Combine flour, baking powder, baking soda, salt and pepper in a large mixing bowl. Stir with fork until evenly distributed, about 30 seconds. Set aside.

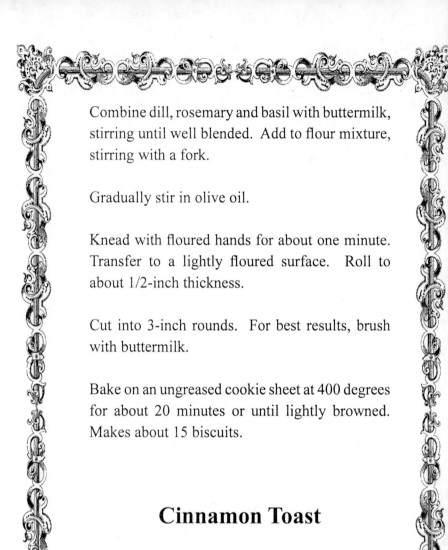

Combine dill, rosemary and basil with buttermilk, stirring until well blended. Add to flour mixture, stirring with a fork.

Gradually stir in olive oil.

Knead with floured hands for about one minute. Transfer to a lightly floured surface. Roll to about 1/2-inch thickness.

Cut into 3-inch rounds. For best results, brush with buttermilk.

Bake on an ungreased cookie sheet at 400 degrees for about 20 minutes or until lightly browned. Makes about 15 biscuits.

Cinnamon Toast

1/2 cup margarine, softened
1 teaspoon cinnamon
1-1/2 teaspoons sugar

Combine ingredients in a medium mixing bowl. Cream with an electric mixer. Spread onto slices of bread. Bake at 400 degrees for about 5-7

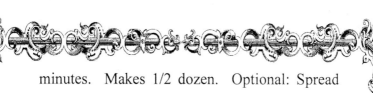

minutes. Makes 1/2 dozen. Optional: Spread onto hot toasted bread. Bake at 400 degrees for about 5-7 minutes. Makes 1/2 dozen. Optional: Spread onto hot toasted bread.

Cherry Vanilla Yogurt

1/4 cup water
1 teaspoon vanilla extract
1 Tablespoon tart cherry concentrate (pg. 113)
2 Tablespoons sugar
1 cup plain non fat yogurt (no xanthan gum)

Combine water, vanilla extract, cherry concentrate and sugar in a small saucepan.

Bring to a boil, then reduce heat to medium and cook for 10 minutes, stirring frequently.

Cool. Fold into yogurt. Makes 2 servings, about 1/2 cup each.

Appetizers and Beverages

Chewy Cheese Puffs

2 eggs, one yolk discarded
8 ounces grated cheddar cheese
1/2 cup flour
1/8 teaspoon paprika
3 Tablespoon margarine, softened
2 dozen pimiento-stuffed olives

Preheat oven to 400 degrees. Lightly mist a cookie sheet with canola oil. Set aside.

In a large mixing bowl with an electric blender, whip egg whites until stiff.

Gradually add yolk, cheese, flour, paprika and margarine.

Blend well, about 2 minutes. Shape into one-inch balls. Indent each ball with thumb, place olive into indentation and reshape into a ball so that olive has been completely covered.

Bake at 400 degrees for about 15 minutes, removing before the cheese balls become browned. Makes 24.

Variation: Omit the olives for plain puffs. These are great, too!

Crunchy Potato Rolls

Filling:
1/2 cup minced onions
1/4 cup water
1 cup cooked russet potatoes, skins removed
1/8 cup skim milk
1 egg white
a pinch of pepper
3/8 teaspoon salt

Dough:
2-1/2 cups flour
1 teaspoon baking powder
1/2 teaspoon salt
3 egg whites
1/2 cup canola oil
2 Tablespoons water

Filling: Saute onions and water in a nonstick saucepan until onions are transparent and water is reduced.

Allow to cool, then combine with remaining ingredients in a medium mixing bowl. Blend with an electric mixer until smooth. Set aside.

Dough: Sift flour, baking powder and salt together. Place in a large mixing bowl.

Make a well in the center of the mixture, then gradually add water, eggs and oil, mixing with a spoon or fork. Knead with floured hands until smooth and non-sticky.

Preheat oven to 350 degrees. Lightly mist a large cookie sheet with canola oil. Roll out dough on a floured surface to a 1/16th-inch thickness.

Cut into 3-inch rounds. Slightly off-center of each round, place 1 Tablespoon of filling.

Moisten edges of dough with water and fold together into half-moon shapes. Press edges together with fingers.

Place with seams facing downward onto cookie sheet, pressing gently in the middle so that each roll resembles a little boat.

Bake at 350 degrees for 30 minutes or until browned and delicately crispy on the outside. Serve warm, or chilled with dip. Makes 2-1/2 dozen.

Cheese Ball

3/4 cup canola oil
1 egg white
1/2 teaspoon Tabasco
1/8 teaspoon salt
2 ounces grated, reduced fat cheddar cheese

Place 1/4 cup of oil in blender with egg white, blend until thick and creamy. Gradually add remaining oil in a steady but thin stream.

Slowly add remaining ingredients. Continue to blend until smooth.

Transfer mixture to a nonstick saucepan. Cook over medium heat, stirring constantly. Mixture will first begin to thicken, then will come away

from the sides of the pan into a sort of ball. Once this happens, remove from the saucepan.

Allow to cool just enough to be able to shape with hands. Shape into a ball. Allow to cool to room temperature before serving.

Squash Puppies

1/4 cup minced onion
2 cloves garlic, pressed
1/4 cup water
2 slices bread, plus water
1/2 butternut squash, cooked (about 2 cups)
3 Tablespoons chopped, dried parsley
1-1/2 teaspoons salt
1/2 teaspoon dried marjoram leaves
1/2 teaspoon paprika
3 eggs, with 2 yolks discarded
3-1/2 cups flour

Preheat oven to 350 degrees. Lightly mist a cookie sheet with canola oil. Set aside.

Saute onion, garlic and water in a non-stick

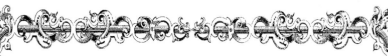

saucepan until onion is transparent and water is reduced. Set aside to cool.

Wet bread with water, then squeeze out and discard water. Combine all ingredients in a large mixing bowl.

Blend with an electric mixer until evenly distributed and a dough forms. Place in 1-1/2 inch balls on cookie sheet and bake for 30 minutes or until browned.

Sandwich Rolls

1 cup Parmesan Eggs recipe *(page 22)*
1 cup shredded lettuce
4 large flour tortillas
4 Tablespoons cream cheese (no xanthan gum)

Divide lettuce and eggs into quarters. Set aside. Cut tortillas into squares. Spread 1 Tablespoon of cream cheese on each tortilla.

On one edge, place a strip of eggs about 2 inches wide, then alongside the eggs, a strip of lettuce about 2 inches wide.

Roll, starting with the egg end.

The cream cheese will work as adhesive to hold the rolls together. Gently slice into 1-inch rolls. Makes 20-24 rolls.

Olive Rolls

4 large flour tortillas
1 cup stuffed olives, minced
2 ounces fresh grated Parmesan
4 Tablespoons cream cheese (no xanthan gum)

Cut tortillas into squares. Spread 1 Tablespoon of cream cheese onto each tortilla.

Sprinkle a quarter of the olives and Parmesan across each tortilla, leaving a one-inch margin along one edge to adhere when rolling.

Roll tortillas, beginning the opposite end of the "margin" edge.

With seam down, slice into 3/4-inch pieces. Makes about 8 slices per roll.

Lemon Slush

1/2 cup lemon juice
3/4 cup sugar
2 cups water
2 cups ice

Combine ingredients in blender. Blend until smooth. Makes 6 servings.

Wild Cherry Slush

One lemon slush recipe (above)
1-1/2 Tablespoons tart cherry concentrate
(page 113)

Add cherry concentrate to blender, mixing until thoroughly blended. Makes 6 servings.

Strawberry Slush Punch

4 cups ice, preferably crushed
1 cup strawberry jelly, seedless
1 cup water

Combine ingredients in blender. Blend until smooth, about 45 seconds to one minute. Makes

12 servings, 1/2 cup each. Variations (1) Replace water with one cup milk, or (2) replace one cup of the ice with one cup yogurt.

Cherry Slush

1/2 cup tart cherry juice concentrate
(see page 113)
1-1/2 cups water
2 cups ice
1/4 to 1/2 cup sugar

Combine cherry concentrate, water, ice and 1/4 cup sugar in blender and mix until smooth. After testing, add remaining sugar if needed. Makes 5 cups.

Cherry Yogurt Shake

1/4 cup tart cherry juice concentrate
(see page 113)
3/4 cups water
1 cup ice
1/8 cup sugar
1/2 cup plain non fat yogurt (no xanthan gum)

Combine in blender and mix until smooth. Makes two 1-1/2 cup servings.

Float Punch

1 recipe Tart Lime Sherbet
(page 89; see below)
1/2 cup sugar
One 12-ounce can frozen pineapple-orange juice
concentrate, thawed
2 liters carbonated water (about 2 quarts plus
1/2 cup), chilled
1 orange

Prepare sherbet according to recipe, adding the 1/2 cup sugar to the amount of sugar used in the sherbet recipe.

Set aside in the freezer in an airtight container.

Combine juice concentrate with carbonated water in a large punch bowl, stirring well but gently.

Top with scoops of sherbet, then slices of orange cut crosswise, peel not removed.

Serve immediately. Makes about 3 quarts.

Dips

Basil Ranch Dip

1/2 cup oil
2 egg whites
1/2 teaspoon salt
1/2 teaspoon sugar
1 teaspoon garlic powder
1 teaspoon onion powder
1/8 teaspoon pepper
1/2 teaspoon dried basil leaves

In medium mixing bowl, combine 1/4 cup of oil and egg whites. Blend with electric mixer until thick and creamy. Gradually blend in remaining oil in a steady but thin stream. Continue adding ingredients until all is well blended. Chill and serve.

Jalapeno Dip

1 fresh jalapeno pepper, chopped
1/4 cup minced onion
6 ounces fat free cream cheese
(no xanthan gum)

Combine ingredients in a small mixing bowl. Blend with electric mixer until evenly distributed. Serve.

Variation: Saute onion and jalapeno first in 1/4 cup of water until water is reduced, then blend with cream cheese.

Onion Dip

1/3 cup minced onions
1/4 cup water
1 clove garlic, pressed
1 cup low fat or fat free sour cream
(no xanthan gum)
a pinch of pepper
3 Tablespoons flour
1/4 teaspoon salt
1/2 teaspoon sugar

Combine onions, water and garlic in a medium nonstick saucepan. Cook over medium high heat, stirring often, until onions are browned and water is gone.

More water may be added if necessary during cooking. Allow to cool.

Combine cooled onion mixture with sour cream and remaining ingredients in a small mixing bowl.

Stir or blend with an electric mixer until all is well blended. Serve chilled.

Garlic and Herb
Cream Cheese Dip

6 ounces fat free cream cheese
(no xanthan gum)
2 sprigs parsley, finely chopped
1 sprig rosemary, finely chopped
3 cloves pressed garlic
1/4 teaspoon salt

Place cream cheese in a medium mixing bowl.

Blend with an electric mixer until well blended.

Sprinkle in remaining ingredients. Continue blending until ingredients are evenly distributed.

Main Dishes

Baked Chilies Rellenos

2 pablano chilies
1/2 cup cooked corn
1/2 cup cooked tomatoes
5 ounces tomato paste
3 ounces shredded, reduced fat cheddar cheese
1 cup skim milk
1 cup flour
2 eggs, one yolk discarded

Cut the chilies in half, lengthwise. Remove pith and seeds. Place skin side up under broiler for about five minutes, or until skin is blistered, but not burned. Skins should easily slip off the chilies and be discarded.

Immediately place chilies into a pot and cover quickly; allow them to self-steam for about ten minutes.

Preheat oven to 350 degrees. Lightly mist an 8 x 8 x 2-inch pan with canola oil. Set aside.

Filling: In a medium mixing bowl, combine corn, tomatoes, tomato paste and 2 ounces of cheese.

Stir gently until evenly distributed. Set aside.

Batter: In a medium mixing bowl, combine milk, flour and eggs. Blend with a whisk until smooth. Set aside.

Fill each of the peppers with 1/4 of the filling, packing in if necessary, then place in pan.

Gently pour batter over the peppers. Batter will overflow into pan.

Bake, covered, at 350 degrees for about 35 minutes, or until batter begins to brown.

Serve with remaining ounce of cheese sprinkled on top. Makes 4 servings.

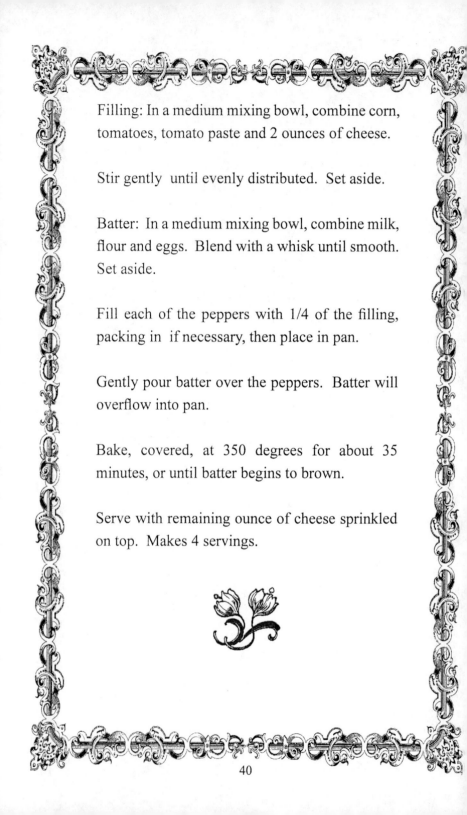

Acorn Squash Souffle

6 eggs
1 acorn squash, cooked and skin discarded
2 Tablespoons flour
1/2 cup skim milk
4 ounces grated, reduced fat cheddar cheese
1/8 teaspoon ground nutmeg
1 small sweet onion, minced (about 3/4 cup)

Preheat oven to 375 degrees. Lightly mist a 2 quart casserole dish with canola oil. Set aside.

Separate the egg whites from the yolks. Place whites in a mixing bowl. Beat with an electric mixer until stiff. Set aside.

Discard three of the yolks. Place remaining yolks in a mixing bowl. Blend with electric mixer until light in color (about 30 seconds).

Continue blending. Add squash, flour, milk, cheese, nutmeg and onion. Blend until smooth.

Fold in the egg whites, and continue to blend briefly until uniform throughout.

Transfer mixture to casserole dish.

Bake at 375 degrees for 40 minutes or until souffle rises and becomes golden brown. Serves 6-8.

Eggplant Italiano

1 eggplant
1 medium onion
1 quart tomato sauce (no meat, no mushrooms)
1 ounce freshly grated Parmesan cheese
1 pound of pasta

Preheat oven to 350 degrees. Lightly mist a 13 x 9 x 2 pan with olive oil. Set aside.

Slice eggplant into slices about 3/4-inch thick. Slice onions as thinly as possible. Set aside.

Place eggplant slices in a layer in the bottom of the pan. Cover with about 1-1/2 cups of sauce. Place onion slices in a layer over the sauce.

Cover with about 1-1/2 cups of sauce. Use remaining sauce to cover any exposed areas.

Sprinkle with cheese.

Bake, covered, for 30 minutes.

While eggplant is cooking, prepare pasta according to package directions.

Serve eggplant over a bed of cooked pasta. Makes 4-6 servings.

Steamed Zucchini Pesto

1 recipe Pesto Sauce *(page 71)*
4 zuchinni squash

Cut zuchinni lengthwise into quarters, then crosswise into 1/2-inch slices.

Steam 15 minutes, gently stirring halfway through.

Top with sauce and fold. Serve hot. Serves four as a main dish, and six to eight as a side dish.

Onion Pie

Crust:
1-2/3 cups flour
3 Tablespoons margarine, softened
3 Tablespoons canola oil
4 Tablespoons water

Filling:
2 pounds onions, minced (about 5 cups)
1-3/8 cups water
2 egg whites
1/2 cup skim milk
1-1/2 teaspoons flour

Crust: Place flour in a large mixing bowl. Cut in margarine with a fork. Continue blending with fork, gradually adding remaining ingredients.

Knead with hands until dough is formed. Shape into a ball and chill. Preheat oven to 400 degrees. Roll dough into an 11-inch circle, about 1/8-inch thick.

Place in pie pan, lining the bottom and sides. Prick holes uniformly in the dough with a fork.

Bake at 400 degrees for 12 minutes or until lightly browned. Set aside.

Combine onions and one cup water in a large nonstick skillet.

Heat on high, stirring often. Allow water to cook completely away and onions to brown, but not burn.

Add 1/4 cup water, stir well, again allowing water to cook completely away and onions to brown.

Add 1/8 cup water, stir well, cooking once more until water has cooked away. Onions should now be uniformly browned. Set aside to cool.

Combine egg whites, milk and flour, blending lightly until smooth. Add to onions, stirring well. Pour mixture into pie shell.

Bake in 400 degree oven for 15-20 minutes or until set. Cool for about 10 minutes before serving.

Serves 4-6 as a main dish, 6-8 as a side dish.

Sour Cream and Onion
Pasta Shells

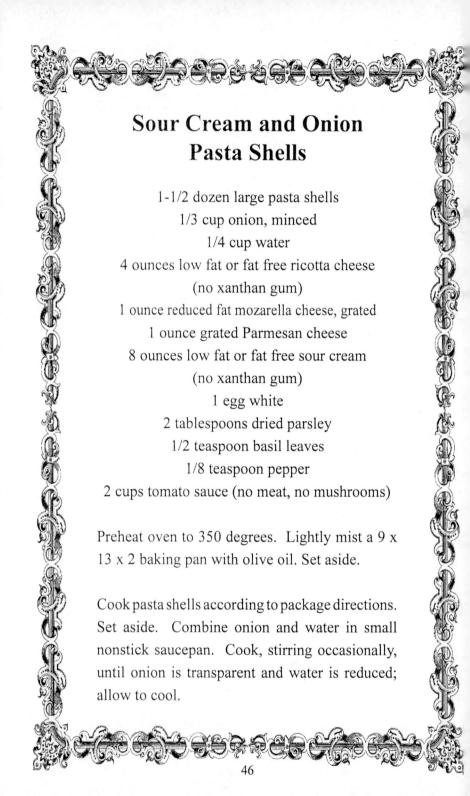

1-1/2 dozen large pasta shells
1/3 cup onion, minced
1/4 cup water
4 ounces low fat or fat free ricotta cheese
(no xanthan gum)
1 ounce reduced fat mozarella cheese, grated
1 ounce grated Parmesan cheese
8 ounces low fat or fat free sour cream
(no xanthan gum)
1 egg white
2 tablespoons dried parsley
1/2 teaspoon basil leaves
1/8 teaspoon pepper
2 cups tomato sauce (no meat, no mushrooms)

Preheat oven to 350 degrees. Lightly mist a 9 x
13 x 2 baking pan with olive oil. Set aside.

Cook pasta shells according to package directions.
Set aside. Combine onion and water in small
nonstick saucepan. Cook, stirring occasionally,
until onion is transparent and water is reduced;
allow to cool.

In a large mixing bowl, combine cooled onions with cheeses, sour cream, egg and spices.

Blend with electric mixer until smooth.

Spoon into pasta shells, placing each into baking pan. Cover with tomato sauce and bake for 45 minutes at 350 degrees.

Allow to cool 10-15 minutes before serving. Makes 6 servings with 3 shells per serving.

Linguine Dijon

8 ounces linguine pasta
1/4 cup water
1/4 cup minced onions
1-1/4 cups skim milk
3 teaspoons flour
1/8 teaspoon freshly gound pepper
1/2 teaspoon salt
3 teaspoons Dijon mustard
1 small tomato, chopped

Prepare pasta according to package directions.

While pasta is cooking, Combine water and onions in a medium saucepan. Cook until water is reduced. Set aside to cool.

Combine milk, flour, pepper and salt in a small mixing bowl. Blend with fork or whisk until smooth.

Add to onions and heat, stirring often. Bring to a boil, then reduce heat to low. Simmer for about one minute. Stir in mustard. Continue stirring until well blended.

Fold into pasta and serve. Makes 2 servings.

Moussaka Casserole

1 eggplant
1/4 cup flour
2 cups skim milk
1/2 teaspoon salt
1/8 teaspoon nutmeg
1/4 cup grated Parmesan cheese
3 eggs, 2 yolks discarded
1-1/2 cups tomato sauce (no meat,
no mushrooms)

Preheat oven to 350 degrees. Lightly mist a 2 quart casserole dish with olive oil. Set aside. Slice eggplant into 1/4-inch slices. Sprinkle very lightly with salt.

Steam 20-25 minutes, or until softened. Set aside to cool.

While eggplant is steaming, make white sauce by blending flour and milk with a whisk until smooth.

Cook in a saucepan over medium-high heat, stirring constantly, until thickened, about 20 minutes.

Stir in nutmeg and Parmesan. Set aside.

Beat eggs with whisk. Continue to beat with whisk, stirring in sauce gradually. Set aside.

Layer eggplant slices and tomato sauce in bottom of casserole dish.

Top with white sauce. Bake at 350 degrees for one hour.

Allow to cool 10-15 minutes before serving. Serves 4.

Vegetable Manicotti in Lemon Sauce

1 dozen manicotti shells (about 1/2 pound)

Filling:

2 egg whites

1 cup low fat or fat free ricotta

(about 7 ounces - no xanthan gum)

1 cup assorted cooked vegetables (such as from

Vegetable Bouillon recipe, *page 63*)

1/2 teaspoon basil leaves

1 Tablespoon dried parsley

1/2 teaspoon salt

1/4 teaspoon thyme

1/2 teaspoon marjoram leaves

1/4 cup flour

Lemon Sauce:

3 cups skim milk

6 Tablespoons flour

1 teaspoon Tabasco sauce

1 teaspoon garlic powder

1/2 teapoon salt

1/4 cup lemon juice

2 Tablespoons prepared mustard

Preheat oven to 350 degrees. Lightly mist a large baking pan with canola oil. Set aside.

Prepare manicotti shells according to package directions. Set aside.

Combine filling ingredients in a large mixing bowl. Blend with electric mixer until smooth. Spoon into shells. Place filled shells into baking pan. Set aside.

Sauce: Combine ingredients in mixing bowl and blend with whisk until smooth. Cook in saucepan over medium heat, stirring constantly, to boiling.

Reduce heat to low and simmer for one minute. Gently pour over pasta shells in baking pan. Bake at 350 degrees for 45 minutes. Serves 6.

Vegetable Pot Pie

Crust:
3-1/3 cups flour
6 Tablespoons margarine, softened
6 Tablespoons canola oil
8 Tablespoons water

Filling:

2 cups skim milk

4 Tablespoons flour

1/2 teaspoon onion powder

1/2 teaspoon salt

1/2 teaspoon garlic powder

1/8 teaspoon pepper

3 cups assorted vegetables[1], chopped, steamed and drained

Crust: Place flour in a large mixing bowl. Cut in margarine with a fork. Continue blending with fork, gradually adding remaining ingredients.

Knead with hands until dough is formed. Shape into two balls and chill. Preheat oven to 350 degrees. Roll one ball of dough into a 12-inch circle, about 1/8-inch thick.

Place in deep-dish 9-inch pie pan, covering the bottom, sides and edge. Prick holes uniformly in the dough with a fork. Set aside.

Combine milk, flour and spices in a medium saucepan. Blend with whisk until smooth.

1. From Foods Allowed list, such as carrots, potatoes, green beans, onions, celery, corn

Cook, stirring often, to boiling. Reduce heat and simmer one minute. Set aside.

Place vegetables in pie pan. Cover with sauce. Roll out remaining ball of pie dough to 1/8-inch. Place on top of pie.

Crimp edges and trim. With a sharp knife, make cuts in dough for ventilation. Bake at 350 degrees for 45 minutes, or until crust is golden brown and sauce is bubbling out of slits.

Serves 4-6 as main dish, 6-8 as a side.

Welsh Rarebit

1/2 cup water
1 egg yolk
2 cloves garlic, pressed
4 ounces low fat, sharp cheddar cheese
1/2 teaspoon mustard
1/8 teaspoon pepper
French bread, sliced and toasted

Combine all ingredients (except bread) in a medium mixing bowl. Stir with whisk until well blended. Place in a nonstick saucepan. Cook,

stirring constantly, over medium-high heat, until cheese is melted. Continue cooking until the mixture thickens, but do not allow it to boil. Serve hot as a dip for the toasted bread. Serves 4-6.

Potatoes in Onion Sauce

1/2 cup water
1 medium onion, minced
2 Tablespoons flour
1 cup skim milk
1/4 teaspoon salt
1/8 teaspoon pepper
1/2 teaspoon chopped, dried parsley
1 pinch paprika
2 large potatoes, cooked, peeled and chopped

Place water and onion in large non-stick skillet. Cook over medium-high heat, stirring often, until onions are transparent and water is gone.

Blend milk and flour with a whisk until smooth. Add to onions. Add salt, pepper, parsley and paprika. Stirring frequently, continue to cook over medium-high heat for about 5 minutes.

Fold in potatoes and continue to cook 5 more minutes,stirring gently. Transfer to a large dish and serve. Serves 3-4.

Variation: Instead of transferring to a serving dish, Place in a mixing bowl. Mash and add 1/2 cup sour cream. Blend well and serve.

Yellow Squash Paprika

1 small onion, minced (about 1/2 cup)
2/3 cup water
1 Tablespoon paprika
1 Tablespoon margarine
2 yellow squash
1 cup fat free sour cream (no xanthan gum)

Slice yellow squash diagonally into 1/8-inch slices. Set aside.

Combine onion, 1/3 cup water, paprika and margarine in large non-stick skillet. Saute until onions are browned and water is gone. Add squash and remaining water. Fold to coat squash with water. Cover and cook 5 minutes.

Uncover and continue to saute until water is gone, and squash and onions are lightly browned. Add sour cream, fold, heat through and serve. Serves 2-3.

Spicy Macaroni and Cheese

1 pound macaroni
1 cup skim milk
2 teaspoons flour
4 ounces reduced fat cheddar cheese, grated
1/4 teaspoon salt
1/2 to 1 jalopeno pepper, finely chopped

Preheat oven to 350 degrees. Lightly mist a 2-1/2 to 3-quart casserole dish with canola oil. Set aside.

Prepare macaroni according to package directions. Set aside.

Blend milk and flour with whisk until smooth. Add to macaroni, stirring well.

Add cheese, salt and jalopeno, stirrring well until ingredients are evenly distributed.

Place in casserole dish, cover and bake at 350 degrees for 30 minutes.

Allow to cool 10 minutes before serving. Serves four.

Tamales

1-1/2 cups corn tortilla flour
1 cup warm water
1/2 cup margarine
1/2 teaspoon salt
1 Picadillo recipe *(page 69)*

Blend flour and water with a whisk. Cover and set aside for about 20 minutes.

Combine magarine and salt in a large mixing bowl. Blend with an electric mixer for about one minute. Mixture will have a fluffy consistency. Add the flour mixture and continue blending until thoroughly combined.

Prepare 12 sheets of aluminum foil, each about 8 x 6 inches in size. Place two level Tablespoons of dough in the center of each sheet.

Press out with fingers to make rectangles about 5 x 3 inches in size, leaving little or no margin of foil against one long edge.

Place one level Tablespoon of picadillo in the center of each dough rectangle, making a lengthwise line from end to end.

Beginning with the no-margin edge, roll in the foil and crimp the ends.

Place rolls in a steamer for 45 minutes. Serve hot or warm. Makes 12 tamales.

***Tamales are traditionally made with corn husks. If you would prefer to use corn husks in place of foil, soak the husks overnight and pat dry before using. Tie the ends with other corn husks.

Squash Casserole

8 ounces wide noodles
1/2 large butternut squash, cooked
(about 2 cups)
1/2 cup skim milk
1/2 cup sweet onions, minced
One egg, plus 1 egg white
1/4 teaspoon salt
1/8 teaspoon pepper
a pinch of dried basil leaves

Preheat oven to 350 degrees. Mist a 2-quart casserole dish with canola oil. Set aside.

Prepare noodles according to package directions, breaking noodles by hand before placing into water to cook. Set aside to cool.

Combine squash, milk, onions, eggs, salt and pepper in a mixing bowl. Blend with electric mixer until well combined. Stir in noodles.

Pack into casserole dish. Sprinkle with dried basil leaves. Cover and cook 35 minutes. Serves 4 as a main dish, 6-8 as a side dish.

Sweet and Sour Eggplant

1/2 small onion, thinly sliced

1/3 small tomato, chopped

1 cup water

1 Tablespoon sugar

1 Tablespoon vinegar

1/8 teaspoon pepper

1 small eggplant, thinly sliced

Saute onion, tomato and 1/4 cup water in a large non-stick skillet.

Once water is reduced, add remaining ingredients (except eggplant), stirring until well combined and sugar is dissolved.

Add eggplant slices. Cover and cook over medium-high heat for about 5 minutes.

Uncover and continue cooking until water is reduced. Serve over rice. Serves 3-4.

Potato Dumplings

1 small minced onion (about 1/2 cup)
1/4 cup water
1 cup cooked potatoes, cut into chunks
1/8 cup skim milk
1 egg white
1/8 teaspoon pepper
1/2 teaspoon salt
1-1/8 cup flour
1 clove garlic, pressed

Saute onion and water in a small non-stick saucepan until water is reduced and onion is transparent. Add more water if necessary, but continue cooking until water is gone. Allow to cool.

Combine with remaining ingredients in a large mixing bowl. Blend with an electric mixer until smooth. Chill in refrigerator for at least 10 minutes.

Drop by teaspoonsful into boiling water. Cook for 3 minutes, or until dumplings rise to top. Makes about 3 dozen.

Soups

Corn Soup

4 ears of fresh corn
2 medium tomatoes
3 cups water
1 small onion, minced
1 teaspoon salt
1/8 teaspoon pepper

Cut corn from cobs, scraping any remaining corn with a large knife, and place in a blender. Set aside.

Place 2-1/2 cups water in a medium saucepan. Bring to a boil. Add the whole tomatoes for about 30 seconds.

Remove the tomatoes carefully from the water. Don't discard the water; reduce heat to low.

Carefully peel tomatoes, remove seeds and chop. Add to the corn in the blender. Add 1/2 cup of the remaining water to the blender and puree.

Add pureed mixture to water in saucepan. Increase heat to medium high. Add onion, salt and pepper.

Bring to a boil, stirring occasionally. Cover, reduce heat to low and simmer for 30 minutes. Serve hot or warm. Serves 4.

Garlic Soup

6 cloves garlic, pressed
4-1/2 cups Vegetable Bouillon (next page)
1/2 teaspoon salt
2 teaspoons dried parsley

Combine ingredients in a large saucepan.

Bring to a boil, reduce heat to medium and cook, stirring occasionally, for 10 minutes. Serve with garlic toast. Serves 4.

Vegetable Bouillon

1 gallon water
1-1/2 teaspoons salt
1 pound carrots, peeled and sliced
1 dozen stalks celery, chopped
1 12-ounce can tomato paste
1 large onion, sliced
1/2 teaspoon pepper
2 cloves garlic

Combine ingredients in a large cooking pot.

Bring to a boil, then cover, reduce to medium-low and simmer for 30 minutes.

Remove vegetables, reserving for a cooked vegetable dish, such as the Variation shown after Blue Cheese over Veggies, *page 65*. Makes about one gallon.

Sides and Sauces

Cheese Potatoes

1 pound cooked potatoes
2 ounces reduced fat cheddar cheese, grated
2 ounces Parmesan cheese, grated
1/2 teaspoon garlic powder
1/4 teaspoon salt
1/8 teaspoon pepper
1/2 teaspoon parsley
1/2 teaspoon oregano

Preheat oven to 350 degrees. Lightly mist an 8 x 8 inch baking pan with canola oil.

Cut potatoes into bite-size chunks and place in pan. Spread evenly. Mist potatoes with canola oil.

Sprinkle remaining ingredients evenly over potatoes: first cheese, then garlic powder, salt and pepper; then parsley and oregano.

Bake at 350 degrees for 30 minutes. Cool about 10 minutes before serving. Serves 4.

Blue Cheese over Veggies

1 zuchinni squash, sliced
1 yellow squash, sliced
1 cup fresh green beens (not bulging)
1 tree of broccoli, chopped
4 ounces blue cheese, crumbled

Preheat oven to 350 degrees. Lightly coat a
13 x 9 x 2 baking pan with canola oil. Set aside.

Place vegetables in a steamer for 10 minutes. Stir
gently, then steam for 10 minutes more.

Transfer to baking pan. Sprinkle with blue
cheese. Bake for 15 minutes at 350 degrees.
Serves 4-6.

Variation: Substitute vegetables with those
remaining from Bouillon recipe *(page 63)*.

Rosemary Potatoes

4 medium potatoes
1/8 teaspoon ground pepper
3 teaspoons dried rosemary leaves
1 teaspoon onion powder
1/2 teaspoon garlic powder
1 teaspoon dried marjoram leaves

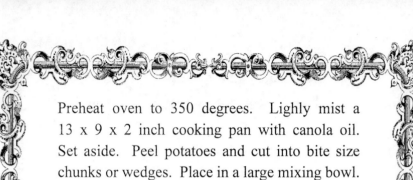

Preheat oven to 350 degrees. Lighly mist a 13 x 9 x 2 inch cooking pan with canola oil. Set aside. Peel potatoes and cut into bite size chunks or wedges. Place in a large mixing bowl. Mist potatoes with canola oil. Add remaining ingredients and toss until spices are evenly distributed.

Spread evenly in pan. Cover and bake at 350 degrees for 45 minutes. Uncover and bake an additional 15 minutes. Serve warm or hot. Serves 4-6.

Variations: Serve with Horseradish Sauce *(page 68)*, or with lemon wedges.

Tomato Rice

1 cup white rice
2/3 cup water
1-1/3 cup tomato juice
1 tomato, chopped
1/2 teaspoon salt
1/8 teaspoon pepper
1/8 teaspoon oregano
1/8 teaspoon basil
2 cloves garlic, pressed
1 Tablespoon margarine

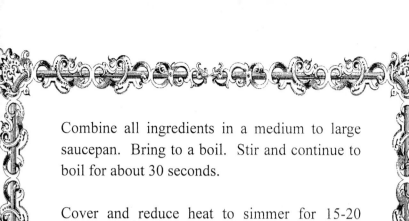

Combine all ingredients in a medium to large saucepan. Bring to a boil. Stir and continue to boil for about 30 seconds.

Cover and reduce heat to simmer for 15-20 minutes or until liquid is absorbed. Remove from heat and leave covered for 5 more minutes.

Serve hot, topped with grated Parmesan or Romano cheese. Serves 3-4.

Baked Macaroni and Cheese

8 ounces macaroni
4 Tablespoons flour
1 teaspoon ground mustard
1/2 teaspoon salt
1/4 teaspoon pepper
3 cups skim milk
2 Tablespoons margarine
1/2 small onion, minced (about 1/3 cup)
6 ounces reduced fat cheddar cheese, grated

Preheat oven to 350 degrees. Lightly mist an 8 x 8 x 2 baking dish with canola oil. Set aside.

Cook and drain macaroni according to package directions. While macaroni is cooking, combine flour, mustard, salt, pepper and milk in a mixing bowl. Blend with whisk until smooth.

Transfer to a medium saucepan. Add margarine. Cook over medium heat, stirring often, until mixture thickens.

Add onions and cheese, stirring until the cheese melts. Set aside.

Place prepared macaroni into baking dish. Cover with cheese mixture. Bake in 350 degree oven for about 30 minutes or until set. Serves 6.

Horseradish Sauce

1 cup skim milk
2 teaspoons flour
1/2 teaspoon salt
1/4 cup finely grated fresh horseradish

Combine milk and flour. Stir with fork or whisk until smooth.

Combine with remaining ingredients in a saucepan.

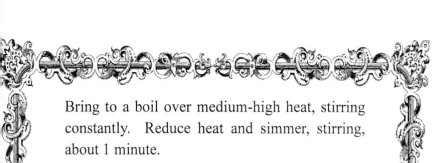

Bring to a boil over medium-high heat, stirring constantly. Reduce heat and simmer, stirring, about 1 minute.

Serve hot or warm over baked potatoes or steamed vegetables.

Variation: After removing from heat, stir in 2 Tablespoons lemon juice.

Picadillo

1 small onion, finely minced
2 cloves garlic, pressed
2/3 cup water
1/8 cup chopped green chilies
1 6-ounce can tomato paste
4 ounces shredded cheddar cheese (reduced fat)
3/4 cup cooked corn
1 Tablespoon chopped dried parsley
1/4 teaspoon salt

Combine onion, garlic and 1/3 cup water in large skillet. Cook, stirring occasionally, over medium-high heat until water has disappeared.

Add remaining ingredients, stir well to combine. Bring to a light boil, reduce heat to low, and cover.

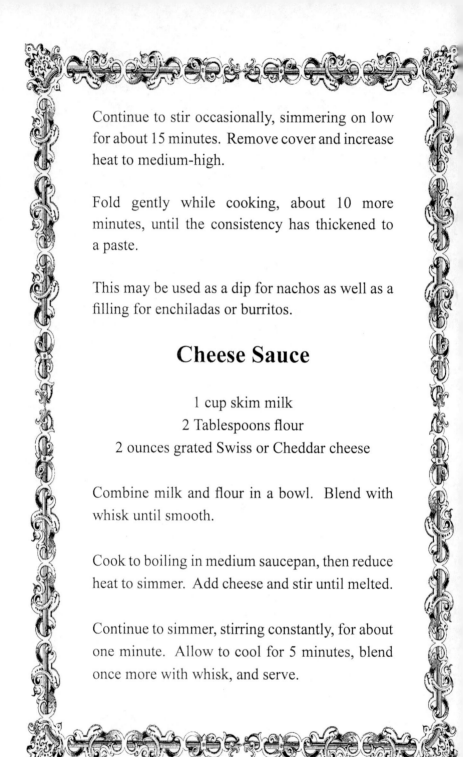

Continue to stir occasionally, simmering on low for about 15 minutes. Remove cover and increase heat to medium-high.

Fold gently while cooking, about 10 more minutes, until the consistency has thickened to a paste.

This may be used as a dip for nachos as well as a filling for enchiladas or burritos.

Cheese Sauce

1 cup skim milk
2 Tablespoons flour
2 ounces grated Swiss or Cheddar cheese

Combine milk and flour in a bowl. Blend with whisk until smooth.

Cook to boiling in medium saucepan, then reduce heat to simmer. Add cheese and stir until melted.

Continue to simmer, stirring constantly, for about one minute. Allow to cool for 5 minutes, blend once more with whisk, and serve.

Pesto Sauce

1/2 cup olive oil
2 Tablespoons dried basil leaves
1/4 cup pine nuts
1/3 cup grated Romano cheese

Combine ingredients in a blender. Puree until appearance is smooth. Toss into freshly cooked pasta or use in pasta salad.

Orange Sauce

1 cup orange juice
2 Tablespoons flour
3 Tablespoons sugar

Combine ingredients in a small bowl. Blend with fork or whisk until smooth and sugar is dissolved. Transfer to small saucepan.

Bring to a boil, stirring frequently, then reduce heat and simmer for about 1 minute. Makes about 3/4 cup.

This recipe is great for desserts - serve warm over ice milk.

French Dressing

1/8 cup vinegar
1/4 cup canola oil
1/8 cup tomato juice
1 Tablespoon chopped dried parsley
1/4 teaspoon salt
1/8 teapoon pepper

Combine ingredients in cruet or mason jar. Cover and shake well until blended. Let sit for 10 minutes before serving.

Blue Cheese Dressing

1 egg white
1 cup canola oil
1/4 cup vinegar
4 ounces blue cheese

Combine egg white and 1/4 cup of the oil in a blender. Blend well.

While still blending, gradually add the remaining oil in a steady, thin stream. Then gradually add the vinegar and 2 ounces of the cheese.

Consistency should be that of a "pourable"

mayonnaise. Stir in the remaining blue cheese in crumbled chunks. Serve chilled. May be used in salad or pasta salad. Consistency may be thinned by adding 1 Tablespoon milk, if desired.

Blue Cheese Dressing II

1 egg white
1-1/4 cup canola oil
1 teaspoon ground mustard
1/2 teaspoon salt
1/2 teaspoon Tabasco sauce
4 ounces blue cheese, crumbled
1/2 cup skim milk
2 Tablespoons lemon juice

In a mixing bowl, whip egg white with electric mixer until stiff. Gradually add canola oil, in a steady, thin stream.

While still blending with mixer, add mustard, salt, Tabasco and 3 ounces of the blue cheese. Gradually add milk and lemon juice, mixing until will blended.

Fold in remaining blue cheese and serve. May be used in tossed salad or pasta salad.

Blue Cheese Vinaigrette Dressing

4 ounces blue cheese, crumbled
1/4 cup vinegar
1/2 cup canola oil
1/8 teaspoon garlic powder
1/8 teaspoon salt
1/8 teaspoon pepper

Combine 2 ounces of cheese with all other ingredients in a cruet or mason jar, shake well until blended. Add remaining cheese and shake well. Shake before serving. May be used in tossed salad or pasta salad.

Lemon Herb Dressing

1 sprig each of rosemary, parsley and dill, chopped
1 basil leaf, chopped finely
2 Tablespoons lemon juice
4 Tablespoons canola oil
1/2 teaspoon garlic powder
1/2 teaspoon onion powder
1/8 teaspoon salt
1/8 teaspoon pepper

Combine all ingredients in a cruet or mason jar.
Shake well. Toss into salad or use in pasta salad.

Hollandaise Sauce

1/2 cup skim milk
1 Tablespoon flour
1 egg, beaten well
2 Tablespoons lemon juice
1/4 teaspoon salt
1/8 teaspoon pepper

Combine milk and flour in a small mixing bowl.
Blend with whisk until smooth.

Transfer to a double boiler. Cook, stirring
frequently with whisk, until thickened.

Stir in egg, continuing to stir with whisk, cooking
until thickened once again.

Add remaining ingredients, stirring until blended.

Serve hot or warm over vegetables, toast or eggs.

Pepper Gravy

2 cups skim milk
2 Tablespoons flour
1/2 teaspoon salt
1/4 teaspoon pepper

Combine ingredients in a medium mixing bowl. Blend with whisk until smooth.

Bring to boil over medium-high heat. Reduce heat to low and continue cooking, stirring occasionally, until thickened, about 3 minutes. Sprinkle more pepper to taste.

Wonderful over biscuits for a biscuits-and-gravy breakfast!

Egg Sauce

1 cup skim milk
2 Tablespoons flour
1/4 cup onion, finely chopped
1/4 cup water
2 hard boiled eggs, one yolk discarded, chopped
1/2 teaspoon salt
1 sprig each parsley and dill, finely chopped

Combine milk and flour in a small mixing bowl. Blend with fork or whisk until smooth. Set aside.

Combine onion and water in medium nonstick saucepan. Cook over medium high heat, stirring well, until onion is cooked and water is reduced.

Add milk mixture and remaining ingredients. Continue cooking, stirring constantly, until boiling, then reduce heat to low.

Simmer for one minute and serve. This recipe is not only delicious, but quite pleasing to the eye. It makes a lovely, elegant dish when served over bread or vegetables.

Pepper Dijon

1/4 cup Tablespoons vinegar
1/2 cup canola oil
4 Tablespoons smooth Dijon mustard
1/2 teaspoon garlic powder
1/4 teaspoon onion powder
1/4 teaspoon pepper

Combine ingredients in a mason jar or cruet and shake until blended. Let sit for at least 15 minutes before serving. Great over escarole and Romaine salad as well as pasta salad.

Salads

Tomato Salad

1 boiled egg, chopped
1 recipe Lemon Herb Dressing *(page 74)*
2 large firm tomatoes, cut into chunks or wedges
1/2 sweet onion, thinly sliced
1/2 cup green olives, sliced or chopped

Combine egg and dressing in a large mixing bowl. Stir well until yolk is smoothly distributed.

Fold in tomatoes, onion and olives. Chill, fold and serve. Serves 3-4.

Corn, Tomato and Celery Salad

4 ears of corn, husks removed
1 bell pepper
3 stalks celery, chopped
1 tomato, chopped
one recipe French Dressing *(page 72)*
1 ounce grated Parmesan cheese

Steam corn, cut from cobs and chill.

Remove seeds and pith from bell pepper and chop.

Place in large mixing bowl. Add tomato, celery and chilled corn. Toss in dressing and cheese. Serves 4-6.

Tropical Fruit Salad

1 apple, cored and chopped
1/2 cup chopped pineapple
1 cup chopped honeydew melon
1/2 cup plain non fat yogurt (no xanthan gum)

Toss ingredients together and serve. Serves 2.

Ranch Pasta Salad

8 ounces pasta
1 boiled egg
1 recipe Onion Dip *(page 37)*

Prepare pasta according to package directions.
Allow to cool.

Chop egg and add to pasta. Stir in onion dip.
Fold until evenly distributed. Serve chilled.
Serves 2-4.

Pasta and Celery Salad

1/2 pound pasta
1 cup chopped celery
1/2 small onion (about 1/3 cup), minced
1 boiled egg, chopped
1/2 cup Blue Cheese Dressing *(page 72)*

Prepare pasta according to package directions.
Allow to cool.

Stir in remaining ingredients. Serve chilled.
Serves 4.

Celery Ranch Salad

1/3 cup Basil Ranch Dip (page 36)
3 boiled eggs, discard 2 yolks, chopped
1 cup chopped celery
1/2 small onion, minced (about 1/3 cup)
1 ounce grated Parmesan

Combine Basil Ranch Dip and eggs in a medium mixing bowl. Stir well. Toss in remaining ingredients. Chill and serve. Makes 2 servings as a main dish, or 4 servings as a pre-meal salad.

Summer Pasta Salad

8 ounces noodles (macaroni, twists or shells)
2 ounces plus 1 Tablespoon canola oil
1/2 tomato, chopped
1/4 cup olives, chopped
1/2 bell pepper, chopped
2 ounces grated Parmesan cheese
1 ounce vinegar
2 boiled eggs, 1 yolk discarded

Cook noodles according to directions on package. Drain, toss with 1 Tablespoon canola oil, and chill. Combine remaining ingredients in a large

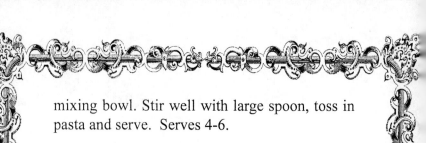

mixing bowl. Stir well with large spoon, toss in pasta and serve. Serves 4-6.

Antipasto Salad

4 large leaves of romaine lettuce
1 bell pepper
1 pound carrots
one dozen radishes
2 ounces reduced fat mozzerella cheese
2 ounces reduced fat cheddar or colby cheese

Wash romaine lettuce leaves and pat dry. Place each leaf of lettuce on a separate salad plate. Set aside.

Remove pith and seeds from bell pepper. Slice thinly. Place one fourth of bell pepper on top of each romaine leaf.

Peel carrots, quarter lengthwise and cut into 2-inch sections. Place one fourth on each romaine leaf. Slice radishes and place on leaves, being sure to arrange the radishes, carrots and bell peppers in a circle.

Cut cheese into small cubes, placing one fourth in the center of each circle. Makes 4 servings.

Chef Salad

1-1/2 cups shredded lettuce
1 boiled egg, sliced
1 stalk celery, halved lengthwise and sectioned
4 cherry tomatoes
1/2 ounce reduced fat cheddar cheese, grated
1/2 ounce reduced fat Swiss cheese, grated
Dressing of your choice

Chef salads are often known for the attractive arrangement of ingredients, as opposed to the "stirred" nature of a tossed salad. They are fun to make and can be quite picturesque.

You may use this guide for your first chef salad, but feel free to experiment with your own ingredients, such as olives, bell peppers, tomato wedges, and even thinly sliced or chopped onions.

Place lettuce in a large serving bowl. Arrange boiled eggs in a circle around the bowl, spacing evenly. Arrange celery sections in a an asterisk shape over the center of the lettuce.

Place tomatoes at "north," "south," "east" and "west" around the edge of the asterisk.

Arrange cheese in little rows or circles around any available space. Serve with dressing on the side. The above recipe is for a complete meal (maybe even with leftovers) for one.

Tropical Rice Ring

6 cups cooked white rice
1 cup crushed pineapple
1 teaspoon ground ginger
1/2 bell pepper, finely chopped
1 egg plus 1 egg white, blended with fork
2 cups shredded lettuce

Preheat oven to 350 degrees. Lightly mist a nonstick ring mold with canola oil. Set aside.

Combine rice, pineapple, ginger, bell pepper and eggs in a large mixing bowl. Stir until evenly coated with eggs.

Pack into ring mold. Bake at 350 degrees for 35 minutes. Edges will brown slightly. Allow to cool completely.

Arrange lettuce on serving plate. Turn rice mixture onto lettuce and serve cold. Serves 6-8.

Desserts

Vanilla Ice Milk

2-1/2 cups skim milk
1/4 cup sugar
1 teaspoon vanilla extract
1/8 teaspoon finely ground vanilla bean

Combine 2 cups skim milk, sugar, vanilla extract and ground vanilla bean in a medium saucepan.

Heat on medium-high, stirring frequently, bringing to a very light boil, then reduce heat to medium.

Stir occasionally, and cook at least 10 minutes to allow the alcohol to cook away.

Remove from heat. Allow to cool, then add just enough milk (about 1/2 cup) to bring the total level to 2 cups.

Once cooled, place in ice cream bucket. Freeze until the desired consistency is reached, 20-25 minutes. Makes about 3 cups.

Flan

1/3 cup plus 1/4 cup sugar
2 egg whites plus 1 egg
1/2 cup skim milk
1 teaspoon vanilla extract

Preheat oven to 325 degrees. In a nonstick skillet over medium-high heat, stir 1/3 cup sugar until melted and a dark brown honey color.

Pour into the bottoms of 4 muffin tins, and set aside. Combine eggs, milk, remaining sugar and vanilla in a mixing bowl and blend with an electric mixer for about one minute, or with a whisk for about 100 strokes.

Pour 1/4 of mixture over the sugar in each muffin tin. Place muffin tins in a pan filled with 1/2-inch of water. Bake at 325 degrees for 45 minutes or until a toothpick inserted in the center comes out clean.

Remove tins from oven. Cool for about 5 minutes. Turn each tin over onto a serving dish and serve. Makes 4 servings.

Melon Sorbet

3/4 cup orange juice
1/4 cup sugar
1 cup chopped honeydew melon
(about 1/4 of a melon)
1 teaspoon lime juice (from about 1/4 lime)

Combine ingredients in a blender. Puree until smooth. Place in ice cream bucket. Freeze until the desired consistency is reached, about 20 minutes. Makes 2-3 servings.

Cookie Dough Crust

1 cup flour
1/4 cup sugar
grated rind of one lemon
1 egg white
1/2 cup margarine, softened

Preheat oven to 400 degrees.

Combine flour and sugar in a medium mixing bowl. Blend with a fork. Add remaining ingredients, blending thoroughly with fork until

a dough forms. Press into a 9-inch pie pan with fingers, being sure to evenly cover bottom and edges. Bake at 400 degrees for 10-12 minutes until lightly browned. Remove and cool.

Cottage Cheese Pie

2 eggs plus 2 egg whites
1/2 cup sugar
1/8 teaspoon salt
1/2 cup skim milk
1 teaspoon vanilla extract
1 cup low fat or fat free small curd cottage cheese (no xanthan gum)
1/4 teaspoon nutmeg
Cookie Dough Crust *(see previous recipe)*

Preheat oven to 425 degrees.

Place egg whites into a large mixing bowl. Beat with an electric mixer until fluffy. Add sugar and continue beating.

Gradually add salt, milk, vanilla, cottage cheese, nutmeg and egg yolks.

Continue blending until evenly distributed.

Due to the curds in the cottage cheese, the mixture will not necessarily be smooth. Place into pie pan with cookie dough crust.

Bake at 425 degrees for about 20 minutes or until a toothpick inserted in the center comes out clean. Makes 8 servings.

Tart Lime Sherbet

2 egg whites
1/3 cup sugar
juice of two limes (about 1/4 cup)

In a medium mixing bowl, whip egg whites with an electric mixer until stiff. Add sugar and continue beating about 2 minutes.

Consistency will be smooth and creamy, but the egg whites will still peak. Gradually blend in lime juice.

Pour into ice cream bucket. Freeze to desired consistency, about 25 minutes.

Store in airtight container in freezer. It will retain a soft consistency.

Double Berry Mint Sorbet

1 egg white
1/2 cup seedless blackberry jam
1 cup mint tea, cooled
1 cup fresh raspberries

Place egg white in a medium mixing bowl. Whip with electric mixer until stiff. Set aside.

In a large mixing bowl, combine jam and mint tea. Blend with mixer until smooth.

Add the egg white, folding until blended.

Pour into ice cream bucket and freeze to desired consistency, about 25 minutes.

Fold in fresh raspberries and serve.

If made ahead of time, sorbet may be stored in the freezer in an airtight container. Fold in raspberriees when sorbet is ready to serve.

Sweet Raisin Curry Rolls

1 egg white
3/4 cup canola oil
1-1/2 Tablespoons curry powder
4 teaspoons sugar
2/3 cup raisins
4 large flour tortillas
2 ounces low fat or fat free cream cheese
(no xanthan gum)

In a medium mixing bowl, beat egg white with an electric mixer until stiff. Continue beating, gradually adding 1/4 cup of canola oil.

Gradually add sugar and curry powder. While still beating, gradually add remaining canola oil at a slow, steady stream, until well blended and creamy.

Add raisins and continue beating for about 30 seconds, or until evenly distributed. Set aside.

Cut tortillas into squares by trimming off the rounded edges. Spread a one-inch line of cream cheese onto one edge of each square (about 1/2 ounce). Over the remaining portion, spread one-fourth of the curry mixture. Beginning at the

opposite end of the cream cheese edge, roll each tortilla, using the cream cheese edge as a final adhesive.

With the sealed edge down, press down with hands to remove any air pockets and to flatten bottom of roll. Cut into 1/4-inch slices. Sliced shapes should be half-moons. Makes about 3-1/2 dozen.

Apricot Date Noodle Pudding

8 ounces wide noodles
3 eggs
1-1/8 cup skim milk
1/2 teaspoon ground cinnamon
1/4 teaspoon nutmeg
1/8 teaspoon ground cloves
1/2 cup sugar
1/4 teaspoon salt
1 dozen chopped dates
1 dozen chopped dried apricots

Prepare noodles according to package directions. Drain and set aside to cool.

Preheat oven to 350 degrees. Lightly mist a

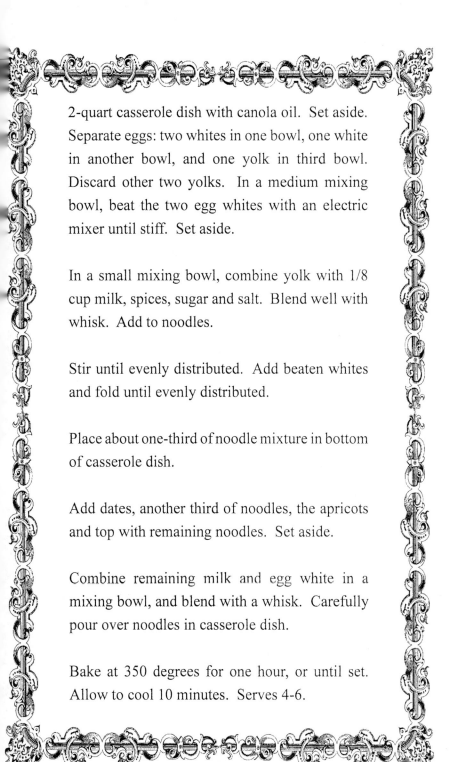

2-quart casserole dish with canola oil. Set aside. Separate eggs: two whites in one bowl, one white in another bowl, and one yolk in third bowl. Discard other two yolks. In a medium mixing bowl, beat the two egg whites with an electric mixer until stiff. Set aside.

In a small mixing bowl, combine yolk with 1/8 cup milk, spices, sugar and salt. Blend well with whisk. Add to noodles.

Stir until evenly distributed. Add beaten whites and fold until evenly distributed.

Place about one-third of noodle mixture in bottom of casserole dish.

Add dates, another third of noodles, the apricots and top with remaining noodles. Set aside.

Combine remaining milk and egg white in a mixing bowl, and blend with a whisk. Carefully pour over noodles in casserole dish.

Bake at 350 degrees for one hour, or until set. Allow to cool 10 minutes. Serves 4-6.

Hot Peaches and Cream

One 1-1/2 ounce box of raisins (about 1/3 cup)
4 large peaches, peeled and halved or sliced
1-1/2 cups skim milk
2 Tablespoons flour
1/2 teaspoon vanilla extract
1/4 cup sugar
nutmeg

Place raisins in a steamer for 10 minutes, then add peaches. Continue to steam for 5 minutes. While steaming, prepare sauce:

Combine milk, flour, vanilla and sugar in a small saucepan. Bring to a boil, then reduce heat to medium.

Cook, stirring constantly, for 10 minutes. Sauce will cook down to about 1 cup. Remove from heat and set aside to cool for about 5 minutes.

Divide peaches and raisins into four serving bowls. Pour sauce on top and sprinkle very lightly with nutmeg. Serves 4.

Strawberry Sherbet

2 egg whites
3/4 cup strawberry jelly
1/4 cup skim milk
2 teaspoons lemon juice

In a medium mixing bowl, beat egg whites with an electric mixer until stiff. Gradually add jelly, milk and lemon juice.

Place in ice cream bucket and freeze until desired consistency is reached. Sherbet may be stored in an airtight container in the freezer. It will retain its soft consistency.

Spiced Fruit

2 apples
1/2 cup chopped dates
one 1-1/2 ounce box raisins (about 1/3 cup)
1 cup water
2 teaspoons sugar
1/8 teaspoon cinnamon
a pinch of nutmeg
a pinch of ground cloves

Peel, core and slice apples. Set aside. Combine remaining ingredients in a saucepan. Bring to a boil, cover and reduce to low.

Simmer for five minutes. Uncover and add apples. Increase heat to medium-high and cook for 3-4 minutes, or until apples begin to soften.

Continue cooking, stirring occasionally, but gently, until the liquid thickens to a syrup. Serve hot or warm, individually or over cake or ice cream. Serves 4.

Cherry Mousse

2 egg whites
1/2 cup sugar
1/4 cup tart cherry concentrate *(see page 113)*

In a medium mixing bowl, beat the egg whites with an electric mixer until stiff. Gradually add sugar.

Continue beating until creamy. Gradually add the cherry concentrate. Refrigerate to chill. Serves 4-6.

Cherry Sherbet

1 egg white
3/8 cup sugar
1/8 cup tart cherry concentrate *(see page 113)*
1/4 cup water

In a medium mixing bowl, beat egg white until stiff. Continue beating, gradually adding sugar, then cherry concentrate, then water. Place in ice cream bucket and freeze until desired consistency is reached. Store in airtight container in freezer. It will retain a soft consistency. Serves 2 to 3.

Whipped Cherry Topping

2 egg whites
1/4 cup water
1/2 cup sugar
1/8 cup tart cherry concentrate *(see page 113)*

In a medium mixing bowl, beat egg whites until stiff. Set aside. Combine remaining ingredients in a small mixing bowl. Stir until the sugar is dissolved. Resume beating egg whites, gradually adding cherry mixture. Great over cake, fruit or pie. Makes about 3 cups.

Orange Sherbet

1 egg white
1 cup orange juice
3 Tablespoons sugar

In a medium mixing bowl, beat egg white with an electric mixer until stiff. Set aside.

Blend juice and sugar about 30 seconds until sugar is dissolved and mixture is frothy. Add the egg whites and continue blending 20-30 seconds until all is well blended.

Freeze in ice cream bucket and freeze until desired consistency is reached. Store in airtight container in freezer. It will retain a soft consistency. Serves 2.

Double Orange Parfait

One recipe Orange Sherbet (above)
One recipe Orange Sauce *(page 71)*
4 teaspoons orange marmalade
4 orange slices (cross-section cuts,
leave on the rind)

In four dessert glasses, place alternating layers of sherbet and sauce. Top each with one teaspoon of marmalade.

Place in freezer to set, about 15 minutes. Do not over-freeze. Garnish each with a slice of orange. Serves 4.

Pie Crust

1-1/4 cups flour
1/2 teaspoon salt
4 Tablespoons margarine
3 Tablespoons canola oil
1/4 cup water

Combine flour and salt in a large mixing bowl. Stir with a whisk about 30 seconds to evenly distribute salt. Work in margarine with a fork.

Gradually add canola oil and water, continuing to blend with fork. Knead lightly by hand, working dough into a ball.

Place in an airtight container or cover with plastic wrap, and chill for about 30 minutes.

Preheat oven to 350 degrees.

Roll dough, on a floured surface, to a thickness of 1/8-inch to 3/16-inch. Trim to fit a 9-inch pie pan.

Gather remainder and roll again. Cut into 3/8-inch strips to use around the edge of the pan. Place dough in pie pan, and press 3/8 inch strips around the edges.

Prick holes in the dough with a fork. Bake at 350 degrees for 10-12 minutes or until lightly browned.

Blackberry Tartlets

One pie crust recipe *(page 99; see below)*
12 teaspoons blackberry preserves

Preheat oven to 350 degrees. Lightly mist a cookie sheet with canola oil. Set aside.

Prepare pie crust dough according to recipe. Roll to 1/8-inch thickness. Cut into 3-inch rounds.

Place 1 teaspoon of blackberry preserve on each round. Fold in half, pressing edges together.

Place on cookie sheet. Bake for 10-12 minutes, or until lightly browned. Makes one dozen.

Strawberry Rhubarb Pie

2 Pie Crust recipes *(page 99; see below)*
2 egg whites
1 cup sugar
3 Tablespoons flour
2 cups (about 3/4 pound) rhubarb, cut into 3/4-inch sections
1 cup strawberries, sliced

Prepare the dough for both crusts, placing one crust in the pie pan as directed. Prick holes with fork, then brush lightly with cold water. Set aside.

Reserve the remaining pie crust dough in the fridge. Preheat oven to 450 degrees.

Beat egg whites lightly with a fork or whisk, about 30 seconds. Add sugar and flour. Continue beating about 30 seconds to 1 minute until smooth. The consistency will be like a paste. Fold in rhubarb and strawberries, continuing to fold until evenly distributed. Transfer to prepared pie crust. Set aside.

Remove remaining pie crust from refrigerator. Roll to 1/8-inch thickness. Place over pie, crimp edges and trim. Cut vent holes in the upper crust. Bake at 450 degrees for about 15 minutes. Reduce heat to 350 degrees, and continue baking for about 30 minutes or until vent holes are bubbling and crust is a golden brown. Allow to cool at least 10 minutes before serving.

Variation: Rather than a solid upper crust with cut vent holes, try cutting 3/8-inch strips, laying crosswise in a lattice design on top. Crimp ends to edge of bottom pie crust dough.

Basics From Scratch

Corn Tortillas

2 cups masa corn flour
1 cup, plus 2 Tablespoons water

This recipe produces a thicker and tastier corn tortilla than those bought off the shelf.

Place flour in a large mixing bowl. Gradually stir in water with a fork.

Knead by hand for about one minute, then separate dough into 8 balls.

Allow balls of dough to set at room temperature for 15 minutes.

Press each ball in a tortilla press between two sheets of wax paper. Each tortilla will be 6 to 7 inches in size. Set aside.

Preheat skillet to medium-high. Gently peel off one piece of wax paper from each tortilla.

Place in skillet with remaining wax paper on top. Gingerly peel off remaining wax paper, then turn after 30 seconds or when edges appear dry.

Cook for 30 more seconds or until tortilla begins to puff. Makes 8 Tortillas.

Variations: Dividing the dough into 12 balls will yield 12 tortillas 5 to 6 inches in size; 16 balls will yield 16 tortillas 4 to 5 inches in size.

Flour Tortillas

2 cups flour
3/4 teaspoon salt
1 teaspoon baking powder
1 Tablespoon margarine, softened
5/8 cup lukewarm water

Combine flour, salt and baking powder in a large mixing bowl. Stir with a fork until well distributed, about 30 seconds.

Gradually add margarine and water, stirring in with fork. Knead by hand for about one minute, shaping into a ball.

Divide the dough into one dozen balls. Cover with plastic wrap and let rest at room temperature for about 15 minutes.

Roll each ball, with a floured rolling pin on a floured surface, to 6-1/2 to 7 inches in size.

Preheat a skillet to medium-high. Cook each tortilla for 1 to 1-1/2 minutes per side. Tortillas should have a lightly browned appearance. Makes 12 tortillas.

No-Egg Pasta

3 cups semolina pasta flour
1 teaspoon salt
2 Tablespoons olive oil
1 cup warm water

Sift flour and salt. Gradually add olive oil and water. Knead with floured hands until soft and pliable, but no longer sticky.

Cover with plastic wrap and chill for at least one hour. Run through pasta machine and allow to dry for one hour.

Boil 3-4 quarts of lightly salted water (about 1/2 teaspoon salt).

Cook pasta for 1-2 minutes or until desired level of doneness is reached. Drain and serve. Makes 4 servings.

Tomato Pasta

3/8 cup warm water
1 teaspoon salt
3 Tablespoons tomato paste
1/4 teaspoon ground sage
2 egg whites
2-3/4 cups semolina pasta flour

Combine water, salt, tomato paste, sage and egg whites in a medium mixing bowl. Blend well with a whisk. Set aside.

Place flour in a large mixing bowl. Gradually stir in liquid mixture with whisk, kneading with floured hands until soft and pliable, but not sticky.

Cover with plastic wrap and chill for at least one hour.

Run through pasta machine. Allow to dry for at least 30 minutes.

Boil 3-4 quarts of lightly salted water (about 1/2 teaspoon salt). Cook pasta for 2-3 minutes or until desired level of doneness is reached. Drain and serve. Makes 4 servings.

Low Fat Yogurt

1 quart low fat milk
5 g yogurt culture *(or as per package instructions; see page 113)*

Heat milk to boiling point, then allow to cool to lukewarm, about 110 degrees. Combine 1/2 cup of milk with yogurt culture, blending until culture has dissolved. Incubate in yogurt maker for 4-5 hours, or until desired consistency is reached. Refrigerate to halt incubation process.

Variations: 1) 3 Tablespoons of prepared yogurt may be used in place of yogurt culture.
2) Yogurt Cheese: Yogurt may be drained in a muslin bag overnight (up to eight hours) prior to refrigerating. Stir in spices and chill.

Low Fat Cream Cheese

2 quarts skim milk
1/4 cup low fat buttermilk

Combine milk and buttermilk in a large bowl. Cover with towel and allow to sit undisturbed, for 24-30 hours, at room temperature. A soft curd will form. Carefully transfer curd into a muslin

Allow to drain overnight (at least 8 hours). Place cheese in an airtight container and refrigerate. Makes about 1-1/2 cups.

Buttermilk

2 quarts skim milk
1/4 cup low fat buttermilk

Combine milk and buttermilk in a large bowl. Cover with towel and allow to sit undisturbed, for 24-30 hours, at room temperature. A soft curd will form. Refrigerate overnight (at least 8 hours), stir and serve. Makes about 2 quarts.

Margarine

3/4 cup butter, softened
3/4 cup canola oil
1/8 teaspoon salt (optional)

Combine ingredients in a blender. Blend well until smooth. Transfer mixture to small air-tight containers. Refrigerate. To serve, remove from refridgerator and let sit at room temperature for about 10 minutes. Makes 1-1/2 cups.

BIBLIOGRAPHY

The information contained in this book was obtained from the following sources:

Aesoph, Lauri M., How to East Away Arthritis, Revised and Expanded, 1996 Prentice Hall

Arthritis Foundation, "Gout," brochure 1999, and "Diet and Your Arthritis," brochure, 1999, Arthritis Foundation, 1330 West Peachtree St., Atlanta, GA USA, (800) 283-7800

"Basic Facts About Processed Free Glutamic Acid (MSG)," Truth in Labeling Campaign Web-site: www.truthinlabeling.org

Biogen Laboratory Developments, LLC, 3189 SE Quail Ln., Gresham, Oregon

Chang, David J., "Of All the Ginned Joints...," Patient Care, March 15, 1996, v.30, n. 5, p. 182(3)

Ellman, Michael, H., M.D., "Treating Acute Gouty Arthritis," The Journal of Musculoskeletal Medicine, March 1992, pp. 71-74

Emmerson, Bryan, T., M.D., Ph.D., Getting Rid of Gout, Second Edition, 2003, Oxford University Press, Victoria, Australia

Emmerson, Bryan T., M.D., Ph.D., "The Management of Gout," The New England Journal of Medicine, v. 334, n. 7, Februaty 1996, pp. 445-451

Flieger, Ken, "Getting to Know Gout," FDA Consumer, v. 29. n. 2, March 1995

Gott, Peter, "Gout May be Related to Medicines," The Dominion Post, April 27, 2001

Harness, T. Angus; Elion, Gertrude B.; Zoellner, Nepomuk, Purine and Pyrimidine Metabolism in Man VII, Part A: Chemotherapy, AATP Depletion and Gout, 1991, Plenum Press, pp3., 139-142, 181, 185-203, 217-221, 227-230, 341-344

Lipetz, Philip, M.D., The Good Calorie Diet, 1994, HarperCollins Publishers, pp. 188-189

Margen, Sheldon, M.D., The Wellness Encyclopedia of Food and Nutrition, 1992, University of CA at Berkeley, Health Letter Associates, pp. 91-94, 348-358

Martinez-Maldonado, Manuel, How to Avoid Kidney Stones, Saturday Evening Post, v. 267, n. 5, Sept.-Oct. 1995, p. 36(3)

MotherNature.com Health Encyclopedia, Low-Purine Diet, http://www. mothernature.com/ency/Diet/Low-Purine_Diet.asp, 1998, HealthNotes, Inc.

National Institute of Arthritis and Musculoskeletal Skin Diseases, "Questions and Answers About Gout," fact sheet, NIAMS Information Clearinghouse, 1 AMS Circle, Bethesda MD 20892-3675, USA, (301) 495-4484

Pennington, Jean A.T., Bowes & Church's Food Values of Portions Commonly Used, Edition 17, 1998 Lippincott-Raven, P. 391

Porter, Roy and Rousseau, G.S., Gout, The Patrician Malady, 1998, Yale University Press

Pritikin, Nathan, The Pritikin Promise, 1983, Simon and Schuster, pp. 110-111

Purine Research Society, 5424 Beech Ave, Bethesda, MD, 20814-1730, USA, e-mail: purine@erols.com, Website: www.purineresearchsociety.org/

Sauber, Colleen M. "Still Painful After All These Years. (gout)," Harvard Health Letter, v. 20, n. 8, June 1995, p. 6(3)

Saunders, Carol S., "Gout: Applying Current Knowledge," Patient Care, v. 32, n. 10, May 30, 1998, p. 125

Souci, S.W.; Fachmann, H.; Kraut; Food Composition and Nutrition Tables, CRC Press, Medpharm, Scientific Publishers, Stuttgart, 2000, 6th Revised and Complete Edition

Steyer, Robert, "Arthritis Suffers Put Up a Spirited Fight Against Chronic Pain," St. Louis Post-Dispatch, Feb 14, 1999

Strange, Carolyn J., "Coping with Arthritis in Its Many Forms, FDA Consumer, March 1996, pp. 17-21

Schwartz, George R. MD, In Bad Taste; The MSG Symptom Complex, Health Press, New Mexico, 1999

Talboth, John H.; Ut, Ts'al-Fan, M.D., Gout and Uric Acid Metabolism, 1976, Stratton Intercontinental Medical Book Corp.

Voijr, F. and Petuely, F. Lebensmittelchemie y. gerichtl. Chemie, 1982, Vol. 36: 73

Wolfram, G. and Colling, M., Z. Ernahrungswiss, 1987, v. 26, pp. 205-13

Zhang, W. et al, "EULAR Evidence based recommendations for gout," Ann Rheum Dis published online 30 May 2006; doi: 10/1136 ard.2006.055269

INDEX

Acorn Squash Souffle, 41
Almond Ginger Biscotti, 20
Antipasto Salad, 82
Appetizers & Beverages, 26
Apricot Date Noodle Pudding, 92
Baked Chilies Rellenos, 39
Baked Macaroni & Cheese, 67
Basics From Scratch, 102
Basil Ranch Dip, 36
Bibliography, 109
Biscotti, Almond Ginger, 20
Biscuits, Buttermilk, 19
Biscuits, Onion and Herb, 23
Blackberry Tartlets, 100
Blue Cheese Dressing, 72
Blue Cheese Dressing II, 73
Blue Cheese over Veggies, 65
Blue Cheese Vinaigrette Dressing, 74
Bouillon, Vegetable, 63
Breakfast, 18
Buttermilk, 108
Buttermilk Biscuits, 19
Casserole, Moussaka, 48
Celery Ranch Salad, 81
Chef Salad, 83
Cheese Ball, 29
Cheese Potatoes, 64
Cheese Puffs, Chewy, 26
Cheese Sauce, 70
Cherry Mousse, 96
Cherry Sherbet, 97
Cherry Slush, 34
Cherry Topping, Whipped, 97
Cherry Vanilla Yogurt, 25
Cherry Yogurt Shake, 34
Chilies Rellenos, Baked, 39
Cinnamon Toast, 24
Converting Fahrenheit to Celsius, 13
Cookie Dough Crust, 87
Corn Soup, 61
Corn, Tomato and Celery Salad, 79
Corn Tortillas, 102
Cottage Cheese Pie, 88
Cream Cheese, Low Fat, 107

Crust, Cookie Dough, 87
Crust, Pie, 99
Creamed Rice, 21
Desserts, 85
Dijon, Linguini, 47
Dijon, Pepper, 77
Dips, 36
Dip, Basil Ranch, 36
Dip, Garlic & Herb Cream Cheese, 38
Dip, Jalapeno, 36
Dip, Onion, 37
Double Berry Mint Sorbet, 90
Double Orange Parfait, 98
Dressing, Blue Cheese, 72
Dressing, Blue Cheese II, 73
Dressing, Blue Bheese Vinaigrette, 74
Dressing, French, 72
Dressing, Lemon Herb, 74
Dumplings, Potato, 60
Egg Sauce, 76
Eggplant Italiano, 42
Eggplant, Sweet & Sour, 59
Eggs, Parmesan, 22
Flan, 86
Float Punch, 35
Flour Tortillas, 104
French Dressing, 72
Fruit, Spiced, 95
Garlic & Herb Cream Cheese Dip, 38
Garlic Soup, 62
Gravy, Pepper, 76
Hollandaise Sauce, 75
Horseradish Sauce, 68
Ice Milk, Vanilla, 85
Jalapeno Dip, 36
Legumes, 9
Lemon Herb Dressing, 74
Lemon slush, 33
Linguini Dijon, 47
Macaroni & Cheese, Baked, 67
Macaroni & Cheese, Spicy, 56
Main Dishes, 39
Manicotti in Lemon Sauce, Vegetable, 50
Margarine, 108

Melon Sorbet, 87
Metric Conversions, 13
Moussaka Casserole, 48
Mousse, Cherry, 96
No-Egg Pasta, 105
Noodle Pudding, Apricot Date, 92
Olive Rolls, 32
Onion Dip, 37
Onion Pie, 44
Orange Parfait, Double, 98
Orange Sauce, 71
Orange Sherbet, 98
Parfait, Double Orange, 98
Parmesan Eggs, 22
Pasta & Celery Salad, 80
Pasta, No-Egg, 105
Pasta Salad, Ranch, 80
Pasta Salad, Summer, 81
Pasta Shells, Sour Cream & Onion, 46
Pasta, Tomato, 106
Peaches and Cream, Hot, 94
Pepper Dijon, 77
Pepper Gravy, 76
Pesto Sauce, 71
Picadillo, 69
Pie, Cottage Cheese, 88
Pie Crust, 99
Pie, Onion, 44
Pie, Strawberry Rhubarb, 101
Pie, Vegetable Pot, 51
Potato Dumplings, 60
Potato Rolls, Crunchy, 27
Potatoes, Cheese, 64
Potatoes in Onion Sauce, 54
Potatoes, Rosemary, 65
Pudding, Apricot Date Noodle, 92
Punch, Float, 35
Ranch Pasta Salad, 80
Rarebit, Welsh, 53
Rhubarb Pie, Strawberry, 101
Rice, Creamed, 21
Rice Ring, Tropical, 84
Rice, Tomato, 66
Rolls, Crunchy Potato, 27
Rolls, Olive, 32
Rolls, Sandwich, 31

Rolls, Sweet Raisin Curry, 91
Rosemary Potatoes, 65
Salads, 78
Salad, Antipasto, 82
Salad, Celery Ranch, 81
Salad, Chef, 83
Salad, Corn, Tomato and Celery, 79
Salad, Pasta & Celery, 80
Salad, Ranch Pasta, 80
Salad, Summer Pasta, 81
Salad, Tomato, 78
Salad, tropical fruit, 79
Salicylates, 10
Sandwich rolls, 31
Sauce, Cheese, 70
Sauce, Egg, 76
Sauce, Hollandaise, 75
Sauce, Horseradish, 68
Sauce, Orange, 71
Sauce, Pesto, 71
Shake, Cherry Yogurt, 34
Sherbet, Cherry, 97
Sherbet, Orange, 98
Sherbet, Tart Lime, 89
Sherbet, Strawberry, 95
Sides & Sauces, 64
Slush, Cherry, 34
Slush, Lemon, 33
Slush, Strawberry, 33
Slush, Wild Cherry, 33
Sorbet, Double Berry Mint, 90
Sorbet, Melon, 87
Souffle, Acorn Squash, 41
Soups, 61
Soup, Corn, 61
Soup, Garlic, 62
Sour Cream & Onion Pasta Shells, 46
Spiced Fruit, 95
Spiced Vanilla Yogurt, 18
Spicy Macaroni & Cheese, 56
Squash Puppies, 30
Strawberry Rhubarb Pie, 101
Strawberry Slush, 33
Strawberry Sherbet, 95
Summer Pasta Salad, 81
Sweet & Sour Eggplant, 59

Sweet Raisin Curry Rolls, 91
Tamales, 57
Tart Lime Sherbet, 89
Tartlets, Blackberry, 100
Toasty Cinnamon, 24
Tomato Pasta, 106
Tomato Rice, 66
Tomato Salad, 78
Topping, Whipped Cherry, 97
Tortillas, Corn, 102
Tortillas, Flour, 104
Tropical Fruit Salad, 79
Tropical Rice Ring, 84
Vanilla Ice Milk, 85

Vegetable Bouillon, 63
Vegetable Manicotti in Lemon Sauce, 50
Vegetable Pot Pie, 51
Veggies, Blue Cheese Over, 65
Vinaigrette Dressing, Blue Cheese, 74
Welsh Rarebit, 53
Whipped Cherry Topping, 97
Wild Cherry Slush, 33
Yellow Squash Paprika, 55
Yogurt, Cherry Vanilla, 25
Yogurt, Low Fat, 107
Yogurt Shake, Cherry, 34
Yogurt, Spiced Vanilla, 18
Zucchini Pesto, Steamed, 43

Lab testing for purine levels in the following foods was provided by Biogen Laboratory Developments, LLC in Gresham, Oregon:

Jicama	Corn Flakes
Okra	Turnips
Beets	Water Chestnuts
Grits	Collard Greens
Broccoli	Xanthan Gum

All items were found to be low in purines at less than 50 mg per 100 g (lowest in purines), with the following exceptions:

1. Broccoli, which was reported at about 71 mg per 100 g. Broccoli was tested both raw and cooked; grits were tested after preparation according to package instructions. Broccoli has remained on the "allowed foods" list, but should be used in moderation.

2. Xanthan gum, often found in dairy products, which was reported to be over 235 mg per 100g (very high in purines).

The tart cherry juice concentrate used in testing recipes was provided by John and Betsy King of King Orchards in Central Lakes, Michigan. More information may be obtained from their website at: www.mi-cherries.com.

The yogurt maker and yogurt cultures were provided (used to test the Low Fat Yogurt recipe on page 103) were provided by VMC Products for Health. More information may be obtained from their website at www.vmc-health.com.

Helpful Links

The tart cherry juice concentrate used in testing recipes was provided by John and Betsy King of King Orchards in Central Lakes, Michigan. More information may be obtained from their website at www.mi-cherries.com or by calling toll-free at 1-877-937-5464.

The yogurt maker and yogurt cultures were provided (used to test the Low Fat Yogurt recipe on page 103) were provided by VMC Products for Health. More information may be obtained from their website at www.vmc-health. com.

Purine Research Society, 5424 Beech Ave, Bethesda, MD, 20814-1730, USA, e-mail: purine@erols.com, Website: www.purineresearchsociety.org/

For additional information on cherry juice concentrate and dried cherries, contact Traverse Bay Farms toll-free at 1-877-746-7477 or visit www. traversebayfarms.com. The company also offers natural (no-sugar added) dried cherries. Free shipping on all dried cherry and case-size cherry juice concentrate orders.

The Gout Hater's Cookbook website, updated on a regular basis, is www. gout-haters.com.

To read more about ordering Gout Hater's Cookbooks, as well as other gout related products, in the United Kingdom and Europe, please visit www. gouthaterscookbook.co.uk

To learn more about the origin of the Gout Hater's Cookbook Collection, please visit the Pittsburgh Post-Gazette at http://www.post-gazette.com/ food/20011104gout1104fnp3.asp

Please visit the website to the Arthritis Foundation at http://www.arthritis. org/

For questions and answers about gout at the National Institutes of Health, please visit http://www.niams.nih.gov/hi/topics/gout/gout.htm

About the Author:

Jodi Schneiter has received degrees in Social Sciences/History and Liberal Arts. Her research and publications center on the fields of gout and low purine foods.